NEW

NATIVE

KITCHEN

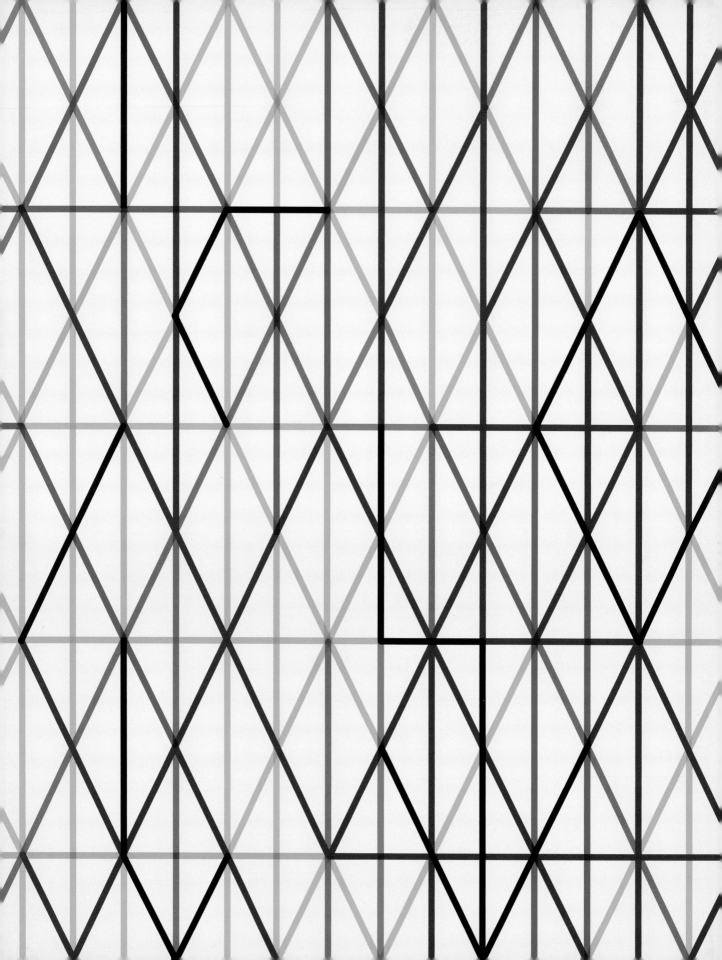

NEW

NATIVE

KITCHEN

Celebrating Modern Recipes of the American Indian

**CHEF FREDDIE BITSOIE
& JAMES O. FRAIOLI**

Photography by Quentin Bacon

Illustrations by Gabriella Trujillo

Abrams, New York

Chapter 5

Introduction

I began experimenting in the kitchen when I was a kid. Maybe it was the PBS cooking shows that I loved, or maybe it was boredom that drew me, but I began to cook in secret when my family wasn't looking. I started out with hamburger patties, working through trial and error—like a culinary detective—to figure out what tasted best. When my mom couldn't find the chicken that she'd placed in the refrigerator one morning, I didn't want to tell her that I'd accidentally set it on fire. Eventually I got better at not burning chicken and learned traditional Navajo (Diné) cooking techniques from my grandmother, through my travels, and from people I met on the way.

I like to say that I grew up everywhere west of the Sandia Mountains, where I was lucky to learn about the plants, animals, and people of different microclimates across the Mojave and Sonoran Deserts. Whenever my family moved to a new town in Utah, Texas, Arizona, or New Mexico, I learned to adapt; I listened closely to the landscape. From my grandmother, I learned that listening to people and places is just as much a part of storytelling as speaking is, and that storytelling is a revered tradition among Indigenous cultures. So I began to listen for the ways that borders like rivers, mountains, rain shadows, or highways influence popular clothing and hairstyles, language and slang, or the food of a specific region.

As a Navajo of the Tábąąhá Edgewater Clan, born for the Nát'oh dine'é Táchii'nii, I loved growing up in the Southwest, where just like my ancestors I breathed in the spicy scent of creosote and petrichor with a sigh of relief each time it rained. To some, the desert might appear barren, dry, and dun-colored. But a closer look reveals that it's bursting with ecologies that dramatically change with every few feet of elevation reaching closer to the clouds.

In a region where water is scarce, I saw the resiliency, and yet the delicacy, of plant species like the saguaro cactus. Their shallow root systems stretch through parched soil to catch whatever moisture they can; they've evolved to thrive in extreme conditions. Blooming brightly, their succulent fruit swells each year despite the summer heat. And so I began to learn that food is the most dynamic way to tell a story. I'm grateful to the desert, and to my grandmother, for teaching me how to listen and how to tell the histories of places and people through my cooking.

Fortunately, I've always enjoyed meeting new people, and that skill helped me fit in whenever I needed to enroll at a new school, make new friends, and learn the culture of a new neighborhood. Later, it continued to help me build long-lasting friendships with members of Native American communities across the continent, many of whom have graciously mentored me and shared their ancestors' culinary wisdom.

As a Navajo, it is imperative that I respect the myriad ingredients cultivated by Indigenous stewards of the land, air, and water in what we now call the United States. And as the executive chef at Mitsitam Native Foods Café in Washington, D.C.'s Smithsonian National Museum of the American Indian, I use that awareness to build varied menus that incorporate sacred Indigenous foodways with reverence.

North America is not, and has never been, a monolith. Just like Europe, it's an expansive continent that's incredibly diverse in terms of language, geography, culture, and more. But European countries like France and Spain are praised for their food traditions, which are taught in elite culinary schools; Indigenous cuisines, with similarly sourced ingredients and finessed preparations, unfortunately don't get the same attention. My aim is to change that.

The land that's now the United States is a land of many nations and communities, with a multitude of cuisines, architectural styles, spiritual beliefs, and languages that make each region uniquely beautiful. Referring to all Indigenous peoples, or their foods, as one homogenous group is like saying that there's no difference between Spain's tapas and France's hors d'oeuvres. At Mitsitam Café, my menus celebrate regional distinctions with thoughtful dishes designed to showcase the rich lakes of the Great Plains, succulent produce of the arid Southwest, lush woodlands of the Northeast, unique botany of the humid South, and teeming bounty of the Pacific Northwest.

With chapters featuring Soups, Salads and Vinai-grettes, Vegetables and Starches, Land and Sea, and Puddings and Sweets, I have worked to make sure dishes are accessible and the recipes easy to follow. I'm especially excited to share the Puddings and

Chef Freddie Bitsoie with food historian Twila Casadore in Papago Park in the Sonoran Desert

Saguaro cactus of the Sonoran Desert

Sweets section, given the common misconception that in pre-Colombian times, Indigenous diets didn't include desserts. Remember, we have always had agave, maple syrup, and sweet biodiverse produce that early Europeans coveted—especially strawberries and other Native fruits.

As you're making the dishes in this book, consider buying ingredients from Indigenous vendors as much as possible, to help support their important work of preserving ancient culinary knowledge and resources. Most of the recipes call for basic ingredients that will be simple to source, no matter where you shop. However, in the Native American Pantry section (page 12), I describe some less common and harder-to-find ingredients. Remember that grocery shopping can be an adventure if you want it to be. Whether you're ordering dried sumac from an Indigenous vendor through Etsy or buying fresh salmon on a road trip along the Pacific Northwest coast, consider it an opportunity to meet new people and learn new things.

In this book, you'll discover that Indigenous foodways are hyperlocal to each region; "farm to table" for millennia. With deep symbiotic roots, there's an interconnected trust between natural resources and the Indigenous communities who have always cared for the land where they live. Consider the three sisters, for example: the North American Indigenous planting method of sustainably growing squash, corn, and beans. Since the 1970s, people have termed the technique "permaculture," but to traditional Indigenous farming practices, it's simply a way of respecting the delicate balance of plants and earth, air, water, and fire.

Alongside these regional recipes, you'll read about many of the ancient communities whose traditions inspired them. I've included general background for these Indigenous cultures throughout the book. By no means is the limited material I provided meant to encapsulate each community or their way of life. It's merely a window into a number of Native Americans and First Nations who are connected with this book through food. I hope you will find their interesting histories and the art that inspired them to be a starting point for further reading and understanding.

The culture and history behind a dish has always been exciting for me to learn about. In fact, that curiosity is what led me to study cultural anthropology and art history at the University of New Mexico. I hadn't planned on becoming a chef, but as my studies progressed, I found myself drawn to research projects about cultural and regional differences expressed through food. One assignment explored the question of why people in New Mexico tend to prefer burgers dressed with chili, whereas diners in Arizona usually request jalapeños. Writing papers like these helped me discover that what I really wanted to do was curate history on the plate. Which is how I ended up in culinary school, and later at the Smithsonian, where I now tell edible stories that allow people to appreciate the living artifact of food.

Through this cookbook, I'm excited to celebrate with you the living history and food artistry of Indigenous nations in North America and the Pacific Islands. This is a snapshot of the continent's ancient ingredients, shown through modernized recipes inspired by ancestral traditions. A hundred years ago, flavor preferences and food trends were tremendously different because food was different. So were our tools. Now we have the convenience of convection ovens as an alternative to underground roasting pits. Once it was common to cook salmon over fire; now we can pan-sear it. Thanks to the internet, we can pair complementary ingredients from regions thousands of miles apart. Of course, trade routes have always sparked cross-cultural exchange, but we live in a more connected age than has ever existed. If we choose, we can use those connections as opportunities to celebrate one another's cultures. And that's how I approach cooking, as an opportunity to honor our past and our diversity. But I'm also not constrained by tradition. Today's Native American cooking, as you'll explore in my recipes to follow, is enriched by vibrant ancestral connections, while also always evolving.

In the kitchen at Mitsitam, unlike my childhood days of secret recipes, I'm surrounded by a team of dedicated chefs who nurture our curated menus. Like the French, who enthusiastically say *Bon appétit!* when sharing a meal, we celebrate in the Native language of the local Nanticoke-Lenape and Piscataway Peoples: *Mitsitam!* Let's eat.

Native American Pantry

Below, you'll find information about some of the less common, possibly unfamiliar ingredients in this book: what they taste like, where to find them, and notes—where relevant—about their fascinating role in Native American cuisine. This isn't meant to be an exhaustive list, but rather a quick primer on foods in my recipes that are specific to the regions where they grow.

Acorn Meal The texture of acorn meal is very similar to almond meal with a nutty, toasty flavor reminiscent of Chardonnay. This flavor profile is because Chardonnay is aged in oak barrels. There are many good online tutorials for leaching out the bitter tannins and roasting acorns before grinding them. It's a lengthy process, however, and you can purchase acorn meal from your local specialty grocer or online.

Agave Nectar Agave nectar tastes like an herbaceous honey. Similar to the way maple syrup is tapped from trees, agave nectar is harvested from the large piña core of a succulent that looks like yucca. It takes around seven years for the agave plant to mature, and the plant dies once it is harvested, so this elixir is a valuable ingredient that should be appreciated. Agave nectar is easy to find at most grocery stores or online, sometimes labeled as agave syrup.

Alaskan King Salmon Alaskan king salmon, also called chinook salmon, are known for their rich flavor and buttery texture. Alaskan king salmon is the largest species of salmon; they can grow to

more than eighty pounds (36 kg) and sixty inches (152 cm) long. You can purchase salmon at most grocery stores, and if you happen to live in the Pacific Northwest, you may live near a community that will sell you a fresh catch directly.

Amaranth Amaranth seeds are similar to quinoa with a sweet and nutty flavor. Amaranth is gluten-free, high in protein and fiber, and health benefits include significant amounts of vitamins A and C. Amaranth seeds can be found in health food stores, grocery stores, and online.

Anaheim Chilies Anaheim chilies are peppers with a mild/medium Scoville Heat Unit level of 500 to 2,500—considerably milder than jalapeños at 2,500 to 8,000. Anaheim chilies turn from green to red as they ripen and can be purchased fresh, roasted, dried, or canned from most grocery stores or online. When the Anaheim chili is dried it turns a burgundy color.

Arrowroot Arrowroot is a gluten-free starch that's dried and ground once harvested from the root of a tropical plant. You should be able to find

Freshly picked golden beets. When cooked, gold beets are smooth and tender with a mild-sweet flavor.

arrowroot in flour form at your local specialty grocery store or online. In a pinch, you can substitute cornstarch for arrowroot.

Aztec Beans First cultivated by the Ancestral Puebloans, Aztec beans are maroon and white, resembling large pinto beans. Aztec beans taste a little sweet and nutty and are well worth the effort of buying online or at a specialty grocer. This variety can be harder to find and is usually only available dried, so you'll need to soak the beans overnight before cooking them.

Banana Leaves Banana leaves are perfect for steaming and gently braising meats but can be difficult to find if you live in a colder climate. Asian grocery stores are a good place to look. If you don't find them in the produce section or frozen aisle, you can order banana leaves online.

Bison Bison and beef can be used interchangeably for nearly any recipe in this book. Bison meat does not taste gamey, but it's sweeter and leaner than beef. Many bison ranches and butcher subscription services offering ethically raised bison have cropped up in recent years. You can also ask your local independent butcher if they sell bison. For the Bison Burgers recipe (page 154), consider using Trader Joe's frozen bison patties for convenience. One thing to be aware of is that bison can become tough when overcooked, because of its leanness.

Blue Cornmeal Blue cornmeal just tastes better. The flavor is more pronounced: the corn tastes richer, sweeter, just better in every way. Many specialty grocers carry blue cornmeal, and it's easy to order online.

Cactus Paddles Cactus paddles, or nopales, are the succulent leaves of the prickly pear cactus or opuntia. They taste like an earthy but tart okra and are packed with nutrients. Before you can eat the cactus, you must remove the thorns. Some people do this by trimming the thorns away with a knife or scissors while holding the paddle leaf with tongs and gloves, others burn away the spines, and still others swear by a boiling method. If you purchase fresh cactus paddles from your local grocery store's produce section, the spines should have already

been removed. There are preserved nopales if you're in a pinch, but I prefer fresh if possible. The brine of jarred cactus paddles dims the fresh flavors that make these worth the effort.

Cedar Berries Cedar berries are similar to juniper berries, although milder with hints of pine and black pepper. If you live near a specialty spice shop, they might carry dried cedar berries or you can search online for a spice vendor and buy them dried.

Cedar Needles or Leaf Tips Cedar leaves, or needles, lend a bright, aromatic forest flavor that reminds me of citrus. The trees' leaves grow in flat, dense clusters and have a flavor profile similar to rosemary. You can buy cedar leaf tips from your local spice shop or order online.

Cherrystone Clams Cherrystone clams are a briny Atlantic shellfish that are both lean and succulent. A good rule to follow is the colder the bay, the more delectable the clams. You can find many local purveyors of cherrystone clams in what's now New England, you can buy them frozen, or you can substitute another type of fresh clam available where you live.

Chokecherry Preserves Chokecherry preserves taste like astringent cherries and are available at farmers' markets, gourmet food shops, and online.

Cholla Buds Cholla buds taste like green beans crossed with asparagus and artichoke hearts. These tender succulents can be harvested between March and May when the cholla cactus flower buds swell, their shades ranging from chartreuse to crimson or lavender depending on the variety and region. Cholla buds can be ordered online, but if you harvest them yourself, make sure to use tongs and remove the thorns by blanching the buds in boiling water or carefully trimming them away.

Fresh cactus paddles, known as nopales, are nutritious and part of the Native American diet.

Beans are an essential staple food
for many Native Americans.

Cranberry Beans A relative of red kidney beans, cranberry beans look like a slightly larger pinto bean, adorned with beautiful mottled cranberry-colored markings. Cranberry beans boast a nutty flavor and creamy texture that will delight. Also called borlotti beans, cranberry beans can be found canned or dried in nearly every grocery store.

Culinary Ash Culinary ash adds a deep smoky flavor to a dish, but traditionally, it has even more versatile uses due to its alkaline properties. If you've ever eaten cornbread and tacos, think about the crumbly texture of cornbread and compare that to the way a corn tortilla tears apart. Through a process called nixtamalization, culinary ash helps the maize, or corn, of your taco's tortilla hold together instead of crumbling apart. You can make your own culinary ash or substitute baking powder. Navajo traditionally burn juniper to produce culinary ash, whereas Hopi typically use a plant called chamisa. There are many different kinds of culinary ash, so if you don't want to use baking powder or make your own ash, you should be able to find a vendor online, such as Blue Corn Custom Designs on Etsy.

Dandelion Leaves The bitter, earthy flavor of dandelion leaves reminds me of radicchio. The flowers are also edible, but all the recipes in this book focus on the leaves. If you don't enjoy the bitterness of dandelions, you can substitute your favorite lettuce or greens of choice.

Dungeness Crab Dungeness crab can grow to about nine inches (23 cm) across, and if you see them in the shallow water, their extremities are a lovely warm orange with subtle shades of purple splashed across the top of their shells. Prized by chefs for their savory, nutty flavor, Dungeness crab are named after what is now called Dungeness Bay, near Sequim, Washington, where the Jamestown S'Klallam community has lived for millennia. If you can't find Dungeness crab where you live, substitute another type of local crab for the recipe. Avoid imitation crab, since this is actually processed fish and will not give you the desired flavor or texture for the dish.

Fiddlehead Ferns Fiddleheads are named for the new leaves of the fern that emerge each spring and unfurl like the curled end of a fiddle. They are a succulent springtime treat that taste like a bright green cross between asparagus and green beans. The Western sword fern (*Polystichum munitum*), ostrich fern (*Matteuccia struthiopteris*), and lady fern (*Athyrium filix-femina*) are good varieties to purchase fresh and eat within two days. It may seem inconvenient to prepare them, but fiddleheads are a wonderful way to mark the end of winter. Make sure to wash the fiddleheads and blanch them in boiling water before cooking. Fiddleheads are a good source of fiber and nutrients, but all good things in moderation: consuming too many fiddleheads has been linked to health complications that range from stomach pain or kidney issues to cancers, so they should be a rare spring treat.

Hearts of Palm Hearts of palm have a wonderfully vegetal flavor and texture that reminds me of asparagus and artichoke hearts crossed with water chestnuts. Just as the name suggests, it's the core of the palm that has been suspended in water. You can find preserved hearts of palm in jars or cans in your grocery store near the canned beans and artichoke hearts. It's difficult to purchase this item fresh.

Hominy Hominy is the ultimate healthy comfort food made from puffed corn kernels removed from their firm outer shells. Through the ancient process of nixtamalization, hominy is corn transformed, emphasizing nurturing flavors like sweet grass and milk. Making your own hominy can be a lot of work, so you can easily purchase canned hominy at your local Mexican grocery store or at larger commercial chains.

Indian Summer Corn Indian Summer corn (*Zea mays*) is a colorful array of sweet kernels that range from yellow to purple, red to deep blue, and everything in between. Growing up in the Southwest, I loved seeing Indigenous vendors selling local corn beneath the expansive blue summertime sky. You can grow Indian Summer corn in many regions if you have access to a garden. Otherwise, you can buy the fresh corn from a local community or grocery store. If this isn't an option where you live, you can substitute the corn that's available at your local grocer.

Jicama Jicama is the deliciously crunchy tuberous root of what is also referred to as a Mexican turnip. The flavor is like a very mild turnip and provides a refreshing lightness like cool cucumbers on a hot summer day. Many grocery store produce sections carry jicama. You just need to peel the root the way you would a beet, then julienne the translucent white vegetable. Jicama can be eaten raw and is a wonderfully healthy snack by itself.

Juneberries Juneberries, or Saskatoon berries, ripen in late June or July across the colder regions of North America. The shrub's fruit tastes like a blueberry and a sweet almond. Juneberries can be purchased frozen if they're not available fresh where you live, or you can substitute blueberries.

Juniper Berries Juniper berries look like teal-hued berries clustered on juniper trees in the late spring and summer, but they are technically small, compact cones. They burst with concentrated flavors and invigorating scents. Different varieties will offer slightly different profiles, but many have an essence of pine. You can purchase juniper berries from specialty spice shops or online.

Manoomin Known to the Anishinaabeg as manoomin or "good berry," this wild rice is a foundation in the foodways and spiritual lives of the Anishinaabeg, Ojibwe, Ojibwa, Saulteaux Chippewa, Ottawa, and other Great Lakes communities. Varieties of native rice that have been cultivated for centuries in the region are more colorful than their commercial white or brown rice counterparts. Flecked with an array of golden hues, manoomin has aromatic grassy flavors that reflect the natural environment of the lakes and prairie. You can purchase manoomin from some communities in the Great Lakes region, shop online, or check your specialty grocery store.

Mexican Oregano Mexican oregano tastes and smells like lemon verbena with an earthy clay undertone. Its deep citrusy scent is like a musky lemon and is quite different from the Italian counterpart that you might associate with pizza sauce. You can purchase dried Mexican oregano at your local grocer or online, or you can try growing a little herb garden on your windowsill and pick the fresh leaves whenever you need to add a depth of flavor with this versatile herb.

Mustard Greens Mustard greens provide a peppery, bitter bite to a dish and can be purchased seasonally from farmers' markets and gourmet grocery stores. If you prefer milder flavors or can't find a vendor to buy mustard greens from, you can substitute kale for a similar texture and more subtle flavor.

Navajo-Churro Lamb Churro lambs are a breed of sheep raised by the Navajo, Hopi, and other communities since the sixteenth century. Because churro lambs are free-range, the meat is appreciated for its succulence, light herbal fragrance, and complex grassy notes. You can purchase churro lamb from many farms and specialty butchers online, such as Heritage Belle Farms or Dot Ranch. Cheviot, Dorset, Rambouillet, and Suffolk sheep are substitutions. Just make sure that the butchered lamb is younger than one year old.

Navajo Steam Corn Navajo steam corn is cooked in its husk over piñon wood embers in a sealed clay oven for ten hours along with five to ten gallons (19–38 L) of water. The resulting corn, infused with the flavor of the piñon, is dried, then later scraped from the cob and used to flavor recipes with the essence of sweet, smoky corn no matter the season. You can purchase this online from Indigenous purveyors including Ben Farms and Blue Corn Custom Designs.

Nopales (see Cactus Paddles)

Pemmican Pemmican, or pimîhkân in the Cree language, also called wasná in the Lakota or Sioux language, is a kind of protein energy bar that has been common in the Great Plains for centuries. It is made from locally available regional meat including dried bison, deer, elk, moose, duck, or beef that is then mixed with berries and nuts, and preserved in tallow. The Lakota and Dakota also prepare a corn-based version. This protein-packed food has become widely popular and is now more available to purchase online, or you can find tutorials to make

Dried sage leaves. As with all dried herbs, store in a sealed container in a cool, dry place. Use within six months for the best flavor.

it at home. This book does not provide a recipe for pemmican or wasná, but I wanted to include a description because it has an important place in the cuisine of the Prairie (what is now called the Midwest) and has been referenced alongside other dishes.

Plantains Plantains are a type of banana that are savory with a more starchy consistency, similar to a yam. You can buy plantains at most Asian or Mexican grocery stores, but many national chain grocers also sell plantains.

Preserved Lemon Preserved lemon provides an explosive punch of citrus and umami flavor that fresh lemons just don't bring to the table. You can preserve your own using kosher salt and spices, but it is easy to buy preserved lemons from a local Middle Eastern grocer, Asian markets, or online if you don't find them at a store near your home.

Prickly Pear Prickly pear fruit tastes like savory plums crossed with watermelon. They are round raspberry-pink orbs that adorn the tops of flat cactus paddles after their blossoms have fallen in the summer. If you gather these yourself, use gloves and tongs, or fire, to carefully cut away the thorns that group in clusters around the outside. The fruit's interior is a dramatic purple succulent with tiny seeds scattered throughout that resemble poppyseeds. If you live in the Sonoran Desert, many grocery stores carry prickly pear jelly, fruit, and juice; however, you should check the label and taste before cooking because these products can include added sugar. You can also purchase prickly pear fruit online.

Quahog Clams Also referred to as chowder clams, quahogs live all along the eastern seaboard from Mexico's Yucatán Peninsula north to Canada's Prince Edward Island. In mudflats, these bivalve mollusks can grow to be four inches (10 cm) in diameter. Their texture can be a little tough, but with some patience, you can cook them to a tender consistency. If frozen or fresh quahog clams are not available at a local grocery store, you can substitute another type of clam.

Queso Fresco Queso fresco is a light cheese that will add a fresh acidic tang. Its texture is similar to ricotta, paneer, or goat cheese. You can purchase queso fresco from Mexican grocers, or most large chains in the specialty cheese section near the deli.

Ramps Ramp bulbs are delicate, wild alliums that grow plentiful in the Southeast. In springtime, depending on your region, you might be able to purchase ramps from the local farmers' market or grocer. If you can't find ramps or if they are out of season, you can substitute green onions combined with garlic for a similar flavor and texture.

Sablefish Sablefish, also known as black cod, lives along the west coast from California to Alaska. The fish has a rich, buttery texture and a high concentration of nutritious omega-3 fatty acids thanks to the cold, deep waters it prefers. You should be able to purchase sablefish from your local grocer, but if it is not available you can substitute Chilean sea bass or cod, although cod will be a much leaner meat.

Sage Sage adds boldness to many Indigenous dishes because of its herbal aroma. Part of the mint family, sage is intensely fragrant and often used to season poultry or add flavor to earthy root vegetables like turnips or parsnips. While fresh sage is preferred, dried sage leaves are equally flavorful and an excellent herb to have on hand.

Saguaro Seeds Saguaro seeds add a delicious nutty crunch. The seeds are very small and black, resembling poppyseeds. Growing up, I loved watching cactus wrens flitting from the top of one towering cactus to another to eat the juicy saguaro fruit and seeds in the summer. If you cannot find a local shop or vendor online that sells saguaro seeds, you can substitute poppyseeds.

Saskatoon Berries (see Juneberries)

Sumac Powder The acidic tang of sumac powder gives a depth of flavor that you will love and want to add to everything from hearty meat dishes to delicate desserts. It should be easy to find ground sumac online, at a local Middle Eastern grocery store, or at a larger chain.

Sunchokes Sunchokes are the tuber root of sunflowers, which are native to North and Central America. Before they're peeled, sunchokes look a little like a brown or tan version of fresh ginger root, and they taste like artichoke hearts crossed with sunflower seeds. If you can't grow or gather your own, many gourmet grocers, farmers' markets, and co-ops sell sunchokes. Otherwise, you should be able to purchase them online.

Tepary Beans Tepary beans are small, nutty, drought-resistant legumes that have been cultivated for thousands of years in the American Southwest. It is easy to order dried tepary beans from an online vendor, but you'll need to build in time to soak them.

Walleye Walleye, also called yellow pike, is a delicate freshwater fish with a buttery texture found in many lakes across North America. Walleye is available to order online and can be found in select fish markets and grocery stores, especially in the Upper Midwest.

Watercress Watercress has a piquant, peppery flavor and can be found at your local gourmet grocery store. It's a refreshing green that grows in wetlands, and its delicate clusters of leaves add a vibrant visual texture to dishes.

Zephyr Squash Zephyr squash is a type of summer squash that's similar to zucchini. Near the stem, the squash is yellow, with green shades at the end where the blossom has fallen off. You should be able to find this at your preferred grocery store or farm stand. Substitute zucchini if you can't find Zephyr squash.

A Native American bounty: cactus paddles (or nopales), prickly pear, and Indian Summer corn

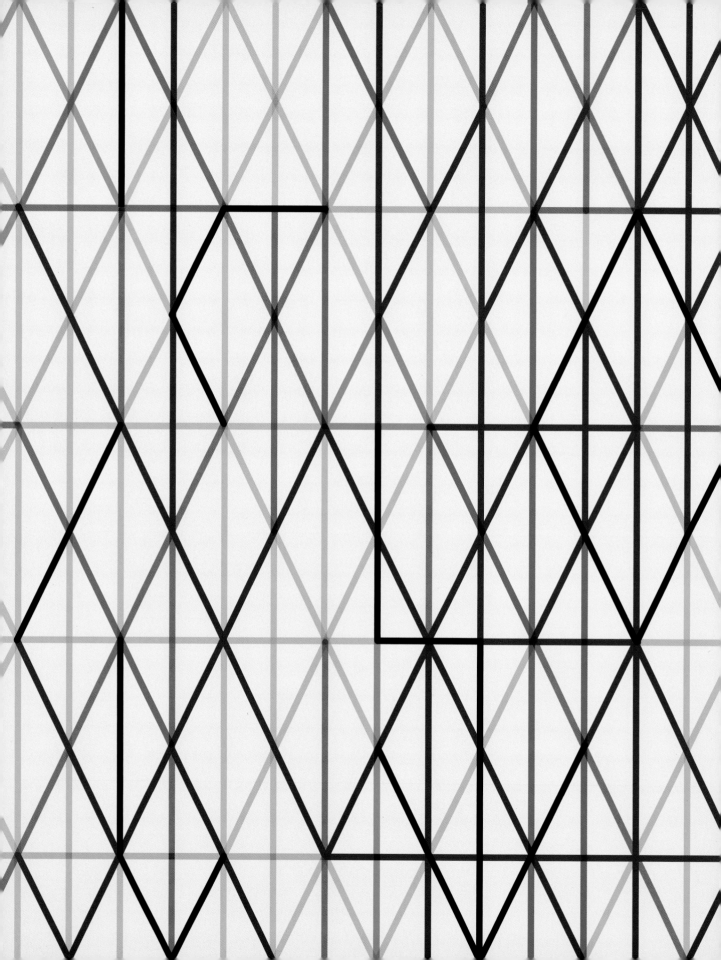

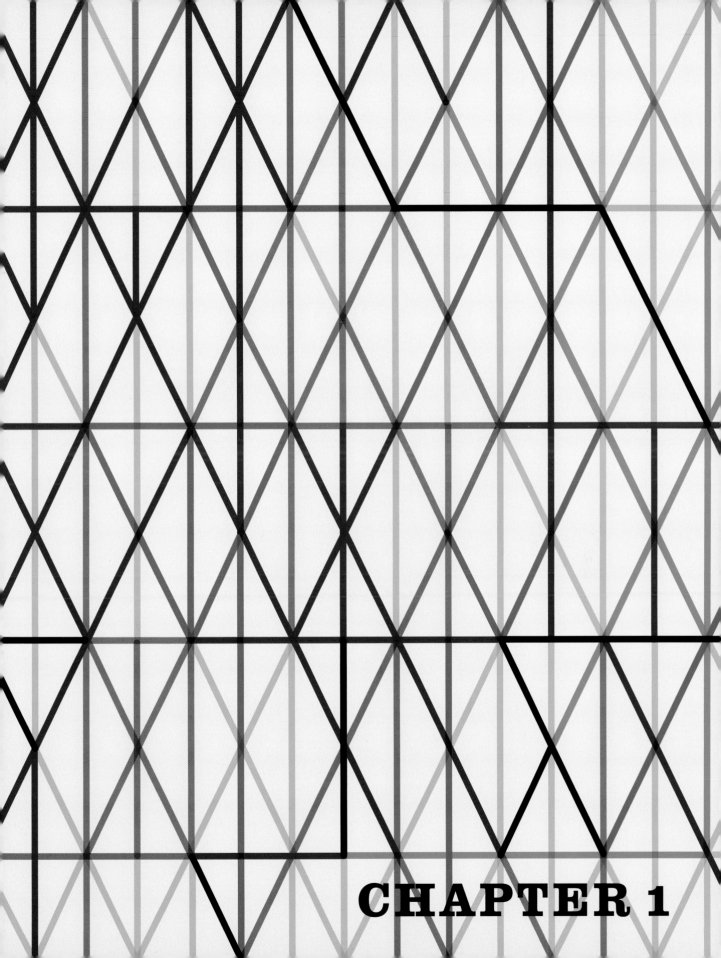

CHAPTER 1

Soups

Acorn Squash and Tepary Bean 28

Aztec Bean and Roasted Green Chili 30

Cheyenne Beef and Sage 36

Forest Acorn 38

Onion, Celery Root, and Parsnip 44

Pinto Bean and Onion 46

Rabbit Stew with Corn Dumplings 48

Red Potato 50

Sweet Summer Corn Broth 52

Three Sisters Bean Stew 54

Wampanoag Cherrystone Clam 58

Soups are just as vital to today's Native American cuisine as they were thousands of years ago when the Kwakawaka'wakw of the Pacific Northwest prepared nourishing seafood soups, the Navajo of the Southwest made hearty squash and bean soups, the Seminoles of the Southeast cooked corn porridge called sofkee, and the Cheyenne created savory stews from the bison roaming wild on the plains.

There's no way for this book to honor the specific recipes of the nearly six hundred Native American communities in what's now the U.S., whose histories date back thousands of years before this country existed. Instead, I've chosen, created, and adapted soups that celebrate some of their shared culinary traditions and honor the sacred, sustaining ingredients that were the staples of many different communities.

Among those ingredients are the three sisters in Native American cuisine. The phrase refers to a planting method that allowed squash, corn, and beans to grow symbiotically and support each other like sisters—each with her own gifts: corn stands tall and straight to provide support for the little bean sister, and squash is sprawling and lush, preventing weeds from invading their garden home. My reverence for those hallowed foods is reflected in my recipes for soups like Acorn Squash and Tepary Bean (page 28) and Sweet Summer Corn Broth (page 52).

Other offerings in this section can be traced back to my own Indigenous ancestry, though everything I understand about my Navajo identity I learned from my travels and the people I've met in my life's journey; those traditions weren't taught in my home or my schools. To honor my ancestors and other Indigenous people of what's now the American Southwest, I've included recipes like Aztec Bean and Roasted Green Chili (page 30). This soup combines ancient traditions with ingredients that are newer to Native cuisine— meaning only centuries old, rather than millennia.

In my recipes, I'm always creating chances for people to think about food differently from what they may be used to. Chances to remember that certain flavors belong together because they've always grown wild together, sharing the same earth and air. I also find ways to be creative within those traditions—taking Indigenous ingredients from thousands of miles apart and building their flavors in ways traditional recipes never could have, given the limits of geography. Travel is important to my life, and that's reflected in my cooking.

The soups that follow are never made; they are built using a systematic, step-by-step approach. For example, the sugars are first extracted from the aromatics, such as onions and juniper berries. Then the pot is deglazed, if needed, followed by the addition of the main ingredients, such as sunchokes, beef, and piñon nuts. Another one of my modern touches is the sparing addition of wheat or dairy when I think it's necessary for flavor or texture, or both. That said, nearly every recipe in this section (and this book) is naturally—or can easily be built to be—gluten- and dairy-free. That's less about catering to food sensitivities than staying true to the foods that were available and plentiful when these recipes were originally created and passed down through story, ceremony, and tradition, carried through hundreds of generations.

I've also given many of these traditional soup recipes modern updates—menus, tastes, and palates evolve, just as accessibility changes: now it's possible for almost anyone, almost anywhere to try my Wampanoag Cherrystone Clam (page 58), not just those who happen to live in the Northeast, near what is now Massachu- setts. Some updates are about taking advantage of modern luxuries, like the blender that gives my Onion, Celery Root, and Parsnip (page 44) a velvety texture that can't be achieved by hand.

Creating these soups for every season, I imagined them as bridges connecting the old and new. They preserve the ancient, sacred spirit of Native American cooking while allowing for its evolution.

ACORN SQUASH AND TEPARY BEAN

During a culinary event at the Tohono O'odham Nation in southern Arizona—the second-largest nation in the U.S.—I was first introduced to the tepary bean. Communities from desert climates have relied on tepary beans since 500 BCE because they're versatile, tasty, and drought resistant; a delicious solution for scarcity in dry times. Tepary beans still grow wild in the southwestern United States and Mexico, and they're readily available at most gourmet groceries and health food stores, or they can be easily ordered online. Navy beans are a good substitute, but it's worth going out of your way to experience the particular flavor of this delicately hearty Native American dish. White varieties of tepary beans are a little sweeter than the earthier brown ones; both are rich and flavorful. Adjust the recipe to your preference, and don't shy away from the acorn squash—it's beautiful as a decorative object, but it's better in soup, where it adds a light, buttery, almost creamy texture.

Serves 4 to 6

3 tablespoons canola oil

1 medium onion, peeled and diced

2 cloves garlic, peeled and minced

1 stalk celery, diced

4 sprigs fresh thyme

1 bay leaf

Salt and freshly cracked black pepper

1 vanilla bean

4 cups (620 g) Cooked Tepary Beans, recipe follows

2 acorn squash, peeled, seeded, and diced

2 quarts (2 L) vegetable stock, or as needed

2 tablespoons crème fraîche, or as needed, optional

2 tablespoons agave nectar, or as needed, optional

COOKED TEPARY BEANS
Makes approximately 8 cups (1.2 kg)

1 pound (455 g) dried tepary beans

2 carrots, trimmed and halved

2 stalks celery, halved

1 medium onion, peeled and halved

Salt and freshly cracked black pepper

In a large, heavy-bottom large pot over low heat, add the oil. When the oil is hot, add the onion, garlic, celery, thyme, and bay leaf. Season with salt and pepper. Split the vanilla bean and, with a sharp knife, scrape the inside of the bean and remove the seeds. Add the seeds to the pot. Sweat the vegetables, stirring occasionally, until they are soft, 10 to 12 minutes. Add the tepary beans and acorn squash and cover with the stock. Add more stock if necessary. Increase the heat to high and bring to a boil. Allow to boil for 5 minutes, then reduce the heat to medium and simmer until the acorn squash is fork-tender, about another 5 minutes. Note: You may need to add more liquid (stock); the beans and squash should be 50 percent of the amount of stock in the pot. Adjust the seasoning if necessary, remove and discard the bay leaf and thyme sprigs, and remove from the heat. Garnish each bowl with 1 teaspoon crème fraîche and 1 teaspoon agave nectar, if using, just before serving. This soup can be refrigerated for three to four days or frozen for four to six months.

In a large pot, add the beans, carrots, celery, onion, salt, and pepper. Cover with water. Bring to a boil over high heat, then reduce to medium and allow to simmer for 1 hour, or until there isn't any bite to the beans. Note: While cooking the beans, keep some additional hot water on hand and add more when the level gets low. Remove from the heat, separate the beans, discarding the vegetables, and set the beans aside until ready to use. Cooked beans can be refrigerated for three to five days.

AZTEC BEAN AND ROASTED GREEN CHILI

This recipe, from the Northern Rio Grande Pueblo, is modernized with unexpected spices but features Aztec beans, first cultivated by the Ancestral Puebloans who lived nearly two thousand years ago in what's now Colorado, Utah, Arizona, and New Mexico. They're large, spotted, maroon-and-white beans that are a little sweet, a little nutty, and a little meaty in texture. Their flavor is much different from the pinto beans they resemble, though they can be harder to find and you'll need to buy them dry, soak them overnight, and cook them from scratch; they're impossible to find in a can. You can substitute canned pinto beans in a pinch; this recipe is forgiving. As for the roasted chilies, some gourmet grocers and farmers' markets sell them, but if you can find chilies fresh at your local market, try roasting your own (see page 32). It's simpler than you might guess, and they'll be the star ingredient of this fragrant, rustic soup.

Serves 6 to 8

3 cups (555 g) dried Aztec beans, soaked in water overnight and drained

1 tablespoon canola oil

5 roasted Anaheim chilies (see page 32), diced

1 large onion, peeled and diced

2 carrots, diced

2 stalks celery, diced

1 teaspoon ground cumin

1 teaspoon ground coriander

2 bay leaves

2 cloves garlic, peeled and minced

2 teaspoons salt

2 teaspoons freshly cracked black pepper

2 quarts (2 L) vegetable or chicken stock, or as needed

6 to 8 teaspoons (30 to 40 ml) sour cream, for garnish, optional

¼ cup (11 g) chives, for garnish, optional

In a medium stockpot, add the beans and 2 quarts (2 L) water and bring to a boil over high heat. Cooking the beans will take at least 2 hours. Keep some additional hot water on hand during the cooking process and add more water if the beans become no longer submerged. The beans are done when there isn't any bite to them. Remove from the heat and drain the beans (do not rinse), keeping the hot bean water. Set both the water and beans aside.

In a separate medium stockpot over low heat, add the oil. When the oil is hot, add the Anaheim chilies, onion, carrots, celery, cumin, coriander, bay leaves, garlic, salt, and pepper. Cook, stirring occasionally, until the onions begin to caramelize, about 30 minutes. Add the cooked beans to the pot and cover the beans with the stock. Add more stock if necessary. Raise the temperature to high and bring to a boil. Cook for about 5 minutes. Reduce the heat to medium-low and simmer for about 20 minutes. You should always have a 2:1 liquid-to-bean ratio; if you need additional liquid, use the reserved bean water. Adjust the seasoning if necessary, remove and discard the bay leaves, and remove from the heat. Garnish each bowl with 1 teaspoon sour cream and some chives, if using, just before serving. This soup can be refrigerated for three to four days or frozen for four to six months.

How to Roast Chilies

Roasting chilies at home is extremely easy. Taking advantage of the chili at its peak of freshness, roasting is also economical and provides a fantastic ingredient that you can use long after the season has passed.

Begin by selecting large, good-quality, mild chilies: consider the Anaheim, poblano, or Hungarian wax. The peppers should be a nice, uniform shade of green—a telltale sign they are mature, ripe, and ready for picking, roasting, and eating. Avoid those beginning to turn color (often reddish-brown). These are overly ripe peppers, and their flesh is generally too sweet at this stage. For any underripe chilies—those picked too soon—place them on the kitchen windowsill and leave them there until they turn that wonderful shade of green. To store before roasting, keep ripe chilies in the crisper drawer of your refrigerator. They should stay fresh for about two weeks.

When you're ready to roast, prepare an outdoor barbecue or grill to high heat. If you want to use your oven, simply preheat the broiler and raise the top rack just under the broiler, or as close as you can get to the heating element.

While the grill or oven is coming up to temperature, wash and dry the peppers. If using the oven, arrange the peppers on a baking sheet lined with aluminum foil.

Place the peppers directly on the grill over the coals or place the baking sheet with the peppers under the broiler. Roast until one side of the peppers is well charred. Turn the peppers over and continue to char. Keep turning until all sides of the peppers are completely charred. Most of the skin should be black at this stage. Depending on what method you're using, the charring process should take

anywhere from 10 to 15 minutes. Just don't char the peppers too long. Burning them completely will result in mushy, disintegrated peppers. We just want to completely char the outer skins.

Once you've achieved the perfect char, remove the peppers from the heat and, while they're still hot, transfer them to a paper bag or heavy-duty zip-top bag and seal. This will allow the hot chilies to steam, which will help loosen the charred skins. Keep the peppers in the sealed bag for 15 to 20 minutes.

Remove the peppers from the bag and, with your fingers, peel away and discard the charred skins. Please don't run them under the faucet. This will ruin the flesh. Take your time and peel. It's okay if you don't get all the skin removed. Leaving a few charred bits is fine.

If you're planning to use the roasted peppers right away, carefully slice open each peeled pepper and scrape out the seeds. Your roasted peppers are now ready.

If you prefer to store the roasted peppers for use later, don't slice them open. Just package them whole in zip-top freezer bags and freeze for up to one year. After you remove them from the freezer and thaw them out, you can split them open and remove the seeds.

Chaco Canyon/
Ancestral Puebloans

Since at least the eighth century, Chaco Canyon has been the ancestral home for many Indigenous peoples, including the Ancestral Puebloans and Navajo. New Mexico's deep, dry canyon in the Four Corners region has evidence of sophisticated irrigation and water diversion channels—a water management infrastructure that made it possible to sustain the large community that grew corn, beans, and squash. The system harnessed the floodwater that comes to desert regions in rainstorms; it's a dangerous undertaking, managing the tide of a flash flood. But also life-saving, if that's your available water for crops.

Chaco Canyon is connected by many ancient roads as well as waterways. For a long time, this was attributed to a robust trade route in the region; however, the architecture of the center—with its many ceremony rooms called kivas—suggests that Chaco Canyon was a religious destination. The nearby sacred site of Chimney Rock also supports that theory. Archaeological discoveries have turned up pottery and stackable vessels for chocolate etched with beautifully intricate geometric designs: evidence that there was likely a lot of trade with Indigenous groups in Central America, where cacao grows wild.

Chaco Canyon is also well known for its ancient adobe homes, some of which were four stories tall. The elaborate villages—built to protect the community from the harsh sun—feature walls adorned with petroglyphs of animals, people, and other symbols. Many underground kivas in the area are still used by modern Puebloan people, keeping their traditions alive. Throughout the intricate maze of rooms, sun dagger symbols pierce spirals to note the seasons, equinoxes, and solstices.

NEW MEXICO'S DEEP, DRY CANYON IN THE FOUR CORNERS REGION HAS EVIDENCE OF SOPHISTICATED IRRIGATION AND WATER DIVERSION CHANNELS—A WATER MANAGEMENT INFRASTRUCTURE THAT MADE IT POSSIBLE TO SUSTAIN THE LARGE COMMUNITY THAT GREW CORN, BEANS, AND SQUASH.

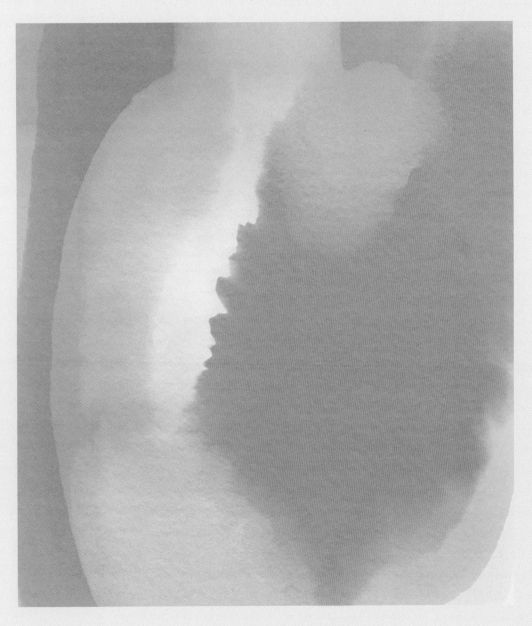

CHEYENNE BEEF AND SAGE

This beef and sage soup is a Cheyenne recipe, created with ingredients from the Great Plains—what's now known as the American Midwest. The Cheyenne are a prairie community whose cuisine reflects what grew wild and what they traditionally hunted—including fresh herbs and bison. Bison were abundant and free-roaming, but eventually cattle began to appear in great numbers, and soon beef took center stage. Inevitably, Cheyenne recipes made the same transition, so this soup calls for beef. For any recipe in this book, you can use bison and beef interchangeably, but you may wish to save bison for grilled dishes or burgers, where the meat is the star; it's expensive and the flavor is more complex. I'd also recommend you choose grass-fed options to reflect the recipe's original flavors. The use of sage is a note any cook can take from traditional Native recipes: sage has a bold enough flavor to complement the intensity of any beef (or bison) dish. Many non-Native home chefs say sage tastes like Thanksgiving or Christmas, but for me and other Natives, it simply tastes like home.

Serves 6 to 8

3 tablespoons canola oil

1 cup (125 g) all-purpose flour

2 teaspoons salt

2 teaspoons freshly cracked black pepper

1 pound (455 g) beef chuck, trimmed and cut into small cubes

1 cup (140 g) diced carrots

1 cup (100 g) diced celery

2 cups (250 g) diced onion

1 tablespoon dried sage leaves

1 bay leaf

4 sprigs fresh thyme

2 quarts (2 L) beef stock, or as needed

3 cups (420 g) diced sunchokes (Jerusalem artichokes) or russet potatoes

½ cup (18 g) chopped fresh sage

¼ cup (13 g) chopped fresh flat-leaf parsley

In a large, heavy-bottom pot over high heat, add the oil. While the oil is heating, season the flour with the salt and pepper. Next, dredge the beef in the seasoned flour. Once the oil is hot, carefully add the beef to the pot and sear until brown on all sides. Note: Do not overcrowd the pot, or you will not achieve a nice sear; you may need to sear the beef in batches. After all the beef is seared, remove from the pot and reduce the heat to low. Add the carrots, celery, onion, dried sage, bay leaf, and thyme. Deglaze the pot with 1 cup (240 ml) of the stock. Return the beef to the pot and add the sunchokes. Cover the beef and sunchokes with the stock. Add more stock to cover if necessary. Increase the heat to medium and bring to a boil. Continue to cook until the sunchokes are fork-tender, about 15 minutes. Remove from the heat and add the fresh sage and parsley. Stir well and adjust the seasoning if necessary. Remove and discard the bay leaf and thyme sprigs and serve immediately. This soup can be refrigerated for three to four days or frozen for four to six months.

FOREST ACORN

This classic Native soup is incredibly simple to build—and while recipes vary from community to community, acorn has always been the predominant ingredient, given its wonderfully rich, nutty taste. Apache (see page 208) communities cooked with acorns gathered from the forests of the southern Colorado Plateau to the southern California mountains for two reasons: they're delicious and a great source of nutrition. On the flip side, they also contain bitter tannins, so they must be cooked before eating—but the acorn meal this recipe calls for has been previously roasted, solving that problem in advance. Many authentic Native American recipes call for water instead of beef stock, and it's true that this soup originated centuries before Spaniards brought cattle to the American continent. But my contemporary take, adding beef stock and beef round, brings an additional depth of flavor.

Serves 6 to 8

3 tablespoons canola oil

1 cup (125 g) all-purpose flour

2 teaspoons salt

1 teaspoon freshly cracked black pepper

2 pounds (910 g) beef round, trimmed and diced

1 quart (1 L) beef stock, or as needed

1 cup (125 g) acorn meal

Fresh parsley, as needed, for garnish, optional

In a large, heavy-bottom pot over high heat, add the oil. While the oil is heating, season the flour with the salt and pepper. Next, dredge the beef in the seasoned flour. Once the oil is hot, carefully add the beef to the pot and sear until brown on all sides. Note: Do not overcrowd the pot, or you will not achieve a nice sear; you may need to sear the beef in batches. After all the beef is seared, return it to the pot and cover the beef with the stock. Consider 1 quart/1 L stock as the base quantity; cooks may need to add more if the stock doesn't cover the ingredients. Bring to a boil, then reduce the heat to medium and simmer until the beef is soft enough to be easily shredded, about 2 hours. Remove the beef, shred, and return to the pot along with the acorn meal. Stir well to combine. Continue to cook for 15 to 20 minutes, then remove from the heat. Garnish with fresh parsley, if desired, and serve. This soup can be refrigerated for three to four days or frozen for four to six months.

Beef vs. Bison— Which Is Better?

When it comes to deciding which red meat to use for my recipes that call for bison or beef, the choice is entirely up to you. Bison and beef can both be part of a healthy diet, and they are equally nutritious and flavorful. Personally, I generally find them interchangeable, although I often reach for beef because it's more available to me and costs less. Other deciding factors that separate the two are environmental conditions and animal husbandry, and bison is considered superior on both of those issues. Also, if you're wanting to stick to traditional Native American cooking, select bison. If you're still unsure, consider the following chart comparing the two. The nutrition stats, according to Onnit Labs, compare a four-ounce (115 g) portion of bison with the same amount of beef, both high-quality top sirloin from grass-fed animals.

	BISON	BEEF
NUTRITION		
Calories	130	140
Protein	25 grams	25 grams
Fat	3 grams	4 grams
Carbohydrates	0 grams	0 grams
ENVIRONMENTAL		
Antibiotics	Not used	Often used
Hormones	Not used	Often used
Carbon Emissions	Low	High
Land	Preserves grasslands	Depletes grasslands

	BISON	BEEF
ANIMAL TREATMENT		
Grazing	Often	Seldom
Feedlots	Seldom	Often (unless "free range")
TASTE		
Flavor	Dry and sweet	Dry and lean (if grass-fed)
PRICE (USD)		
Retail	Expensive; $9 or more per pound for most cuts	Less expensive; $6 to $7 per pound for most cuts

Cheyenne

The Cheyenne, or Tsitsistas in their language, are a group of communities from the Greats Plains of the Midwest. Traditionally farmers, they gathered wild foods and hunted animals including elk, porcupine, prairie dog, bison, and antelope. After horses were introduced, transportation over long distances across the plains became much easier, and today equestrian culture is a pivotal part of Cheyenne life.

The community is known for its pottery, in part because the high-quality clay of the prairie is so plentiful. Many Cheyenne ceramics depict the movement of wind dancing upon sacred grasses. Cheyenne beadwork is also an important part of the culture, adorning baby cradles and traditional clothing, as well as jewelry and shoes. Today, the beads are often glass or acrylic—but it's still common for Cheyenne artisans to create their designs the ancient way, using colorful seeds.

For entertainment, the Cheyenne and other Great Plains communities played hoop and pole. Think of it as a much harder version of darts, with a moving target. The large hoop is made with a web of ropes woven across the center. Different colors and symbols delineate point values, just like a dartboard. One person rolls the hoop and the player must expertly launch a pole through the hoop. Where it lands inside the web determines the score; the highest score wins the game.

Traditional Cheyenne cuisine is very protein rich. Dried bison meat was incorporated in most dishes, flavored with wild herbs from the grasslands. The Cheyenne food tradition is also noteworthy for creating one of the world's first energy bars, a preserved snack called pemmican. Some versions are made with corn, but more typically it's made from ground jerky mixed with tallow, herbs, fruit, and berries. There are many recipes online for pemmican, if you want to make it at home; it's become more popular in recent years as a healthy snack to grab on the way to the gym, or for a long hike.

TRADITIONAL CHEYENNE CUISINE IS VERY PROTEIN-RICH.
DRIED BISON MEAT WAS INCORPORATED IN MOST DISHES, FLAVORED
WITH WILD HERBS FROM THE GRASSLANDS.

ONION, CELERY ROOT, AND PARSNIP

This authentic Native American soup invites you to appreciate the earthy root vegetables, herbs, nuts, and berries that were—and still are—staples in many Indigenous cuisines. It also modernizes those ingredients with a texture upgrade. Coconut milk—essential to Indigenous cuisines of the Caribbean and Pacific Islands—adds a little sweetness and a smoother consistency. In this recipe, we'll forgo the traditional method of mashing soup ingredients and embrace the blender. This soup is best with a silky quality, which you simply can't get without blending. Visit your local farm stand, community garden, or the organic section of your grocery store to find the freshest vegetables. And if you want to dress up this soup even further, garnish with a colorful drizzle of black bean or red beet puree.

Serves 6 to 8

¼ cup (60 ml) canola oil

1 celery root, cleaned and diced

1 large onion, peeled and diced

4 parsnips, diced

3 juniper berries, ground

2 teaspoons dried sage leaves

1 bay leaf

1 stem fresh rosemary

Salt and freshly cracked black pepper

2 quarts (2 L) vegetable or chicken stock, or as needed

1 cup (240 ml) coconut milk

2 tablespoons chopped fresh sage or parsley

¼ cup (35 g) chopped piñon nuts, optional

In a large, heavy-bottom pot over low heat, add the oil. Once the oil is hot, add the celery root, onion, parsnips, juniper berries, dried sage, bay leaf, and rosemary. Season with salt and pepper. Sweat the onions, stirring occasionally, until they are soft, about 10 minutes, then deglaze the pot with 2 cups (480 ml) of the stock (note: the liquid will continue to evaporate while the onions soften). Continue to cook until the onions are nice and soft, about 10 minutes; do not burn. Adding more stock a little at a time will prevent this while continuing to deglaze the pot; scrape up any brown bits that have stuck to the bottom of the pot before they burn. When the onions become caramelized, add the remaining stock to just cover the vegetables and herbs. Note: You may have stock left over; you can use this to thin the soup if necessary. Increase the heat to high and bring to a boil. Boil until the celery root is fork-tender, about 20 minutes. Remove from the heat and discard the bay leaf and rosemary. Carefully transfer the soup to a blender (do not overfill) and puree in batches (caution: contents will be hot). Puree for about 5 minutes, or until an extremely smooth consistency is achieved. You want all the pulp to be liquefied. Strain and return the pureed soup back to the pot. If the soup is too thick, add a little stock to thin it out. Reheat on low and adjust the seasoning if necessary. Stir in the coconut milk just before serving and garnish each bowl with some chopped herbs and piñon nuts (if using). This soup can be refrigerated for three to four days or frozen for four to six months.

This recipe comes from my mother, who'd craft pinto bean and onion soup from the onions she picked at a farm in the town of Cortez in southwestern Colorado. The secret is to use fresh herbs and homemade stock, and to sweat the onions thoroughly. They're the heart of this soup. Take your time, let them go well beyond translucent, and stop cooking just before they caramelize. You want them soft and sweet, without any bite. I love the creamy, earthy, well-rounded flavor of pinto beans in this dish; they complement the onions perfectly. If you're looking for a frugal recipe that tastes like a splurge, you've found it here. And for me, it's also a trip back in time.

Serves 4 to 6

3 tablespoons canola oil

1 medium onion, peeled and diced

1 stalk celery, diced

2 bay leaves

5 sprigs fresh thyme

3 (16-ounce/455 g) cans pinto beans, drained and rinsed

Salt and freshly cracked black pepper

2 quarts (2 L) chicken or vegetable stock

½ cup (20 g) chopped fresh cilantro

In a large, heavy-bottom pot over low heat, add the oil. Once the oil is hot, add the onion, celery, bay leaves, and thyme. Sweat the onions, stirring occasionally, until they are very soft, about 10 minutes. Add the beans and season with salt and pepper. Stir well and add the stock. Increase the heat to high and bring to a boil. Boil for 5 minutes, then reduce the heat to low and allow to simmer until the liquid is reduced by one-quarter, about 15 minutes. Adjust the seasoning if necessary, remove and discard the bay leaves and thyme sprigs, and remove from the heat. Garnish each bowl with fresh cilantro on top. This soup can be refrigerated for three to four days or frozen for four to six months.

RABBIT STEW WITH CORN DUMPLINGS

This recipe comes from the Southeastern Cherokees of northern Georgia and the Carolinas, though it's not specific to the region. Corn dumpling soups are popular among many Native communities. If you've eaten chicken and dumplings or hush puppies, you're already familiar with the basic idea—but rabbit will offer a slightly more intense, rich, and savory taste. Chicken is a fine substitute. Try not to think of this recipe as a new version of something you already love, but rather a centuries-old tradition that's inspired dozens of now-familiar American recipes. (And for good reason—it's incredibly tasty.)

Serves 6 to 8

⅓ cup (75 ml) canola oil

4 skin-on bone-in rabbit legs

4 skin-on bone-in rabbit thighs

1 tablespoon salt

1 tablespoon freshly cracked black pepper

1 medium onion, peeled and diced

2 carrots, diced

2 stalks celery, diced

2 bay leaves

5 sprigs fresh thyme

2 quarts (2 L) chicken stock

Corn Dumplings, recipe follows

20 ramp bulbs, cleaned and trimmed

2 cups (40 g) loosely packed spinach leaves

CORN DUMPLINGS
Makes 20 to 24 dumplings

4 ears corn, kernels removed

1 cup (125 g) all-purpose flour

½ cup (60 g) yellow cornmeal

½ teaspoon salt

In a large, heavy-bottom pot over high heat, add the oil. Season the rabbit with the salt and pepper. Once the oil is hot, carefully add the rabbit to the pot. Sear until brown on all sides. Note: Do not overcrowd the pot, or you will not achieve a nice sear; you may need to sear the rabbit in batches. After all the rabbit is seared, remove from the pot and set aside. Reduce the heat to low. Add the onion, carrots, celery, bay leaves, and thyme to the pot and cook until the onion is soft, about 10 minutes. Deglaze the pot with 2 cups (480 ml) of the stock, scraping up any brown bits from the bottom. Return the seared rabbit to the pot and add the dumplings, ramps, spinach, and the remaining stock. Increase the temperature to high and bring to a boil. Once boiling, reduce the temperature to medium, cover, and allow to simmer for 25 to 30 minutes, or until the rabbit and vegetables are tender. Adjust the seasoning if necessary and remove and discard the bay leaves and thyme sprigs. Remove from the heat and serve immediately. This soup can be refrigerated for three to four days or frozen for four to six months.

In the bowl of a food processor fitted with the dough blade, add the corn kernels, flour, cornmeal, salt, and 1 cup (240 ml) water and process until a dough is formed. If the dough seems dry, add a little more water. (Note: If you do not have a processor, a mortar and pestle will work. Grind the corn first before adding the flour, cornmeal, salt, and water.) Next, knead the dough into a smooth ball, then place the dough ball into a bowl and cover with a kitchen towel for 15 minutes. To form the dumplings, roll out the dough on a floured surface as thin as you can. Then using a knife or pizza cutter, slice the dough into thin strips, about ½ inch (12 mm) wide and 3 inches (7.5 cm) long. Set the pieces aside until ready to use.

RED POTATO

Centuries before potatoes arrived in North America, Native Americans had been cultivating sunroots, also called sunchokes or Jerusalem artichokes. But potatoes eventually made their way to North America and into Native American cuisine. This simple but elegant potato soup originates from the Seminole community in what's now Florida (see page 88). They'd have used white potatoes, but my version calls for the red thumb potato, a relatively new fingerling with brilliant red skin and pink-red flesh. They're beautiful to look at, almost like a red core daikon radish; they have a creamy, buttery taste; and they hold up well—especially in comparison to russets, which can disintegrate in soups. You can't go wrong with bacon, potatoes, and fresh herbs—and this updated take on an ancient recipe is no exception.

Serves 6 to 8

3 strips bacon, diced

1 medium onion, peeled and diced

3 stalks celery, diced

2 cloves garlic, peeled and minced

2 bay leaves

5 sprigs fresh thyme

½ teaspoon vanilla extract

2 teaspoons salt

2 teaspoons freshly cracked black pepper

2 pounds (910 g) red thumb potatoes, halved lengthwise

2 quarts (2 L) chicken stock, or as needed

¼ cup (11 g) chopped chives

In a large, heavy-bottom pot over low heat, add the bacon and render the fat, being careful not to burn the bacon. Once the bacon is fully cooked, remove from the pot, drain on a paper towel–lined plate, and reserve. Next, add the onion, celery, garlic, bay leaves, thyme, vanilla, salt, and pepper to the bacon fat. Cook for about 10 minutes, stirring occasionally, until the vegetables are soft. Add the potatoes and cover the potatoes with the stock. Add more stock to cover if necessary. Increase the heat to high and bring to a boil. Once boiling, immediately reduce the heat to medium so as to not break apart the potatoes. Simmer while reducing the liquid until the potatoes are fork-tender, about 8 minutes. Remove the bay leaves and thyme sprigs, remove from the heat, and garnish with the chives and bacon bits just before serving. This soup can be refrigerated for three to four days or frozen for four to six months.

SWEET SUMMER CORN BROTH

This broth is one of my signature dishes, prepared in summer at the height of the season, and saved for the last night of the year. When I was a kid growing up on reservations, this sweet summer corn broth was always warm on the stovetop when friends and family stopped in on New Year's Eve. We'd have a bowl or two to celebrate what had passed, or what was to come. It's a tradition I still continue with my friends and family, and maybe you will too. You can use yellow or white corn, frozen or fresh, but to build it like I do, you must start in the summertime, when super sweet Indian Summer corn is fresh and just harvested. The yellow, white, red, or purple colors intensify as the kernels cook so your soup looks, and feels, like a celebration. Build it, freeze it, and share it with the people you love. Note: You can also add small pieces of salmon or chicken, if desired.

Serves 6 to 8

6 fresh ears sweet Indian Summer corn, kernels removed and cobs reserved

½ cup (70 g) frozen corn

1 medium onion, peeled and roughly chopped

3 stalks celery, roughly chopped

3 carrots, roughly chopped

3 cloves garlic, peeled and minced

2 bay leaves

Salt and freshly cracked black pepper

Fresh thyme leaves, for garnish

In a large pot, add 4 quarts (3.8 L) water, corn and cobs, frozen corn, onion, celery, carrots, garlic, bay leaves, and salt and pepper. Bring to a boil over high heat, then reduce the heat to low. Simmer for 3 hours, then remove from the heat and strain the liquid through a fine-mesh sieve, discarding the vegetables. Line the sieve with a paper towel and strain the broth again, for clarity. Return the strained broth to the pot and place over medium heat. Reduce the broth by three-quarters, then season with a little more salt and pepper, to taste. Garnish with fresh thyme. Serve hot or warm. This soup can be refrigerated for three to four days or frozen for four to six months.

THREE SISTERS BEAN STEW

Earlier in this book, I spoke about how beans, corn, and squash are considered the three sisters of Native American cuisine, a reference to their planting method. But what's notable about Indigenous recipes isn't so much what we cook or how we cook it, but our relationship with it. These spiritual connections have always been honored and reflected in ceremonies and dances, one of which is the Bean Dance, vital to the coming-of-age ceremony for Hopi children. The dance involves a hope for rain and a promise of sustenance and productivity— though the details are kept close, sacred to the community. Recipes like the one below are more than a rustic taste of Native America; they're an aspect of spirituality, culture, and community. Keep that in mind as you prepare this comforting stew, best served with grilled or roasted meats, or spooned over wild rice for a delicious vegetarian dinner. I prefer the combination of kidney, cannellini, and black beans, but substitute what you have or what you like: pinto, Great Northern, or cranberry. If you like a little heat, add roasted chilies (see page 32). Their smoky spice pairs beautifully with the sautéed onions and garlic.

Serves 4 to 6

2 tablespoons canola oil

1 small onion, peeled and diced

2 cloves garlic, peeled and minced

2 sprigs fresh thyme

1 bay leaf

½ carrot, peeled and finely diced

½ stalk celery, finely diced

Salt and freshly cracked black pepper

1 cup (177 g) cooked kidney beans

1 cup (155 g) cooked cannellini beans

1 cup (185 g) cooked black beans

½ cup (90 g) diced tomatoes

2½ cups (600 ml) chicken or vegetable stock

In a large, heavy-bottom pot over medium heat, add the oil. When the oil is hot, add the onion, garlic, thyme, bay leaf, carrot, and celery. Season with a pinch each of salt and pepper and allow the ingredients to cook, stirring occasionally, until the onion is soft and translucent, about 5 minutes. Add the cooked beans, diced tomatoes, and stock. Bring to a light boil, then reduce the heat to low and simmer for several minutes; the stock will thicken. Adjust the seasoning if necessary, remove the thyme sprigs and bay leaf, and serve hot. This stew can be refrigerated for three to four days or frozen for four to six months.

Hopi

The importance of water in Hopi culture is seen repeatedly in artwork depicting rain clouds. Life in the desert can be difficult, but the Hopi are talented agriculturists who developed techniques for dry farming in northeastern Arizona using natural precipitation like winter snow and summer monsoon floods. They were, and still are, a people acutely attuned to changes in the soil, weather, wind, and water. These are delicate balances that the Hopi solemnly respect—and they celebrate the beauty that comes from the meditative work of living in a harsh climate.

Even with the limited water resources of an arid region, Hopi crops thrive. Beans, squash, sunflowers, onions, and pumpkins are common, as well as cotton, tobacco, and domesticated turkeys. As with many Native American cultures, Hopi spirituality is connected to the food they cultivate. Corn is central to all aspects of Hopi life, with a spiritual place in the culture like a nurturing mother. It's incorporated into recipes including hominy, cornbread, and stews or chili. You'll find many foraged Hopi ingredients in this book's recipes, including cactus fruits, wild greens, and piñon nuts.

According to Hopi beliefs, we now live in the fourth world, which is called Tuuwaqatsi. Before a great destruction or disaster in the third world, Grandmother Spider guided the people who had good hearts. In one legend, Grandmother Spider set a reed between the worlds for the Hopi to walk through; many accounts say that the opening to the fourth world is the Grand Canyon.

Another vital aspect of Hopi spirituality are kachinas, protective ancestral spiritual guardians. The kachinas are like earth spirits that are similar to the relationship some cultures have to elves, or the Shinto kami. In ceremonies throughout the year, dancers depict different kachinas, performing in town squares in the spring and summer and, in winter, in sacred prayer spaces called kivas. It's also common for dolls to be carved in the kachinas' likenesses, then adorned in traditional clothing and regalia.

LIFE IN THE DESERT CAN BE DIFFICULT, BUT THE HOPI
ARE TALENTED AGRICULTURISTS WHO DEVELOPED TECHNIQUES
FOR DRY FARMING.

WAMPANOAG
CHERRYSTONE CLAM

When I was young, my parents passed down stories of Native communities who lived along the Pacific and Atlantic coasts and harvested fresh clams as a staple of their recipes: steamers, cherrystones, and quahogs. After meals, they'd gather the shells for later use: tools, utensils, currency, and decoration. Nothing was wasted. Hundreds of years later, what still remains is the tradition of harvesting the freshest clams possible to re-create traditional Native dishes. This soup originates from the coastal Wampanoag people, who lived in what's now New England, and this recipe is the inspiration for what's now known as New England clam chowder. With this soup, you'll create an experience that tastes deliciously familiar—but skips the heavy cream. It relies instead on fresh-shucked clams and sunchokes for its comforting heartiness.

Serves 6 to 8

1 tablespoon canola oil

1 small onion, peeled and chopped

2 cloves garlic, peeled and minced

1 small leek, cleaned and julienned

½ teaspoon dried thyme

1 bay leaf

Salt and freshly cracked black pepper

3 pounds (1.4 kg) sunchokes (Jerusalem artichokes), peeled and diced

2 russet potatoes, peeled and diced

3 cups (720 ml) clam stock, or as needed

1¾ cups (205 g) freshly shucked cherrystone clams, roughly chopped

In a large, heavy stockpot or Dutch oven over medium heat, add the oil. When the oil is hot, add the onion, garlic, leek, thyme, bay leaf, and salt and pepper. Cook until the vegetables are soft, stirring occasionally, about 5 minutes. Add the sunchokes, potatoes, and clam stock. Add more stock to cover if necessary. Bring to a boil then reduce to a simmer. Cook until the sunchokes and potatoes are tender, about 30 minutes. Add the clams and a little more stock if the liquid is low. Cook for another 5 minutes, remove and discard the bay leaf, then remove the pot from the heat. Adjust the seasoning if necessary and serve immediately. This soup can be refrigerated for three to four days or frozen for four to six months.

Wampanoag and Haudenosaunee

The Wampanoag and Haudenosaunee are a group of Native Americans from the Northeast and adjacent islands. Traditional homes in the region are dome-shaped, which is ideal for insulating against the snow and ice in winter. Larger meetings take place in longhouses, where there's more room for decisions to be discussed with the community. In fact, *Haudenosaunee* can be translated as "people of the longhouse." The French named them Iroquois, but members of the community prefer Haudenosaunee or the name of their specific community, such as the Kanien'kehaka (Mohawk).

Corn, fish, and hunted game are staples of the ancestral diets of the region's Indigenous communities. But cranberries also play an important role. The Wampanoag word for cranberry is *sasumuneash*, and they along with their Haudenosaunee neighbors celebrate an annual cranberry festival. Every October during harvest, as the community prepares for the winter months, children are given the day off from school. They go down to the bogs to hear elders tell passed-down stories about the history of the cherished fruit—like the ancestor fishermen who packed cranberries on their boats for long fishing trips. The vitamin C in the tiny, red, nutrition-packed morsels prevented the fishermen from getting sick on their journeys.

Although the cranberry harvest involves a lot of work, it also includes many celebrations and ceremonies thanking the Creator for the bounty. Plus, after all that effort, everyone is hungry and looking forward to relaxing together at the feast. Many families bring dishes to share, including cranberry crisps, cranberry sauce, and cranberry cobbler; others play drums and sing. To honor their traditions in this book, I've included a delicious Rice Pudding with Cranberry (page 266). The tangy acidity of cranberries is a great pairing with a rich, hearty main course—or as a way to brighten roasted vegetables or spring salads.

THE WAMPANOAG WORD FOR CRANBERRY IS *SASUMUNEASH*,
AND THEY ALONG WITH THEIR HAUDENOSAUNEE NEIGHBORS
CELEBRATE AN ANNUAL CRANBERRY FESTIVAL.

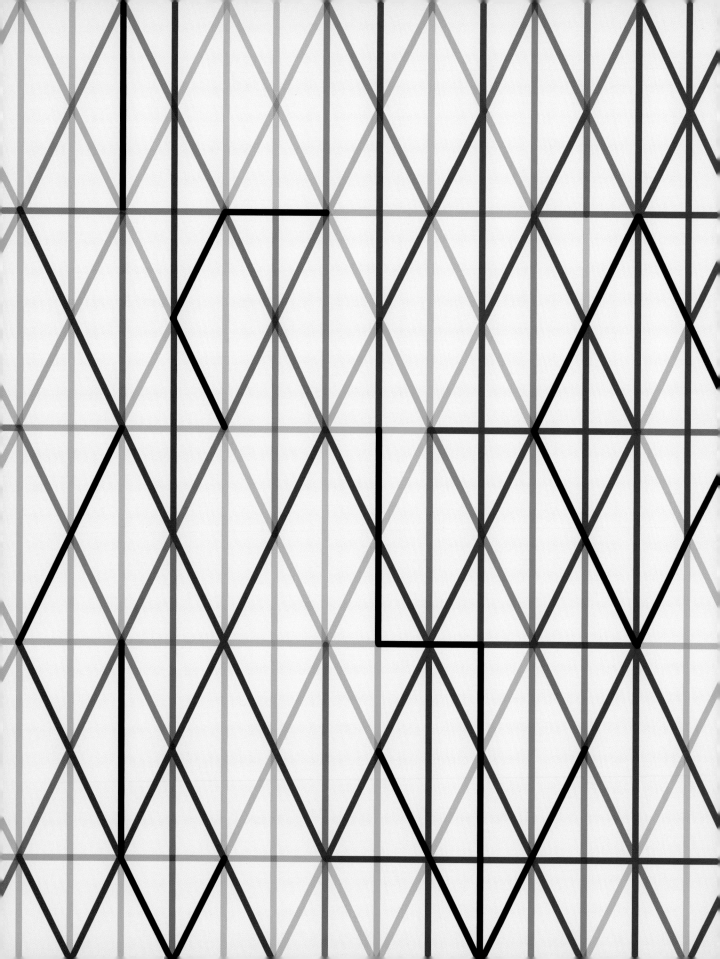

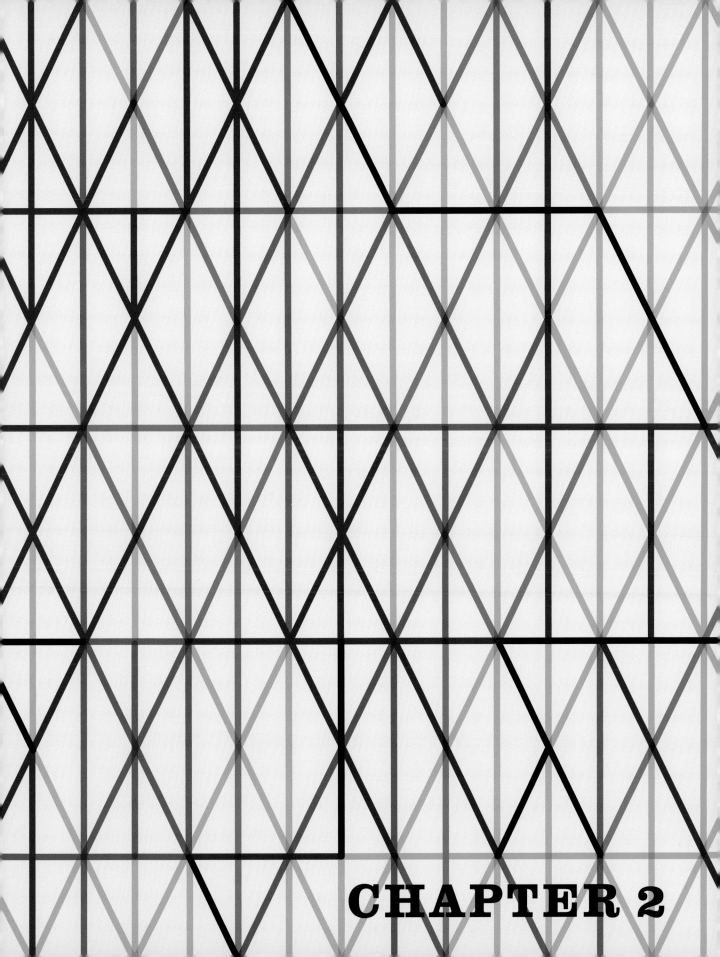

CHAPTER 2

Salads and Vinaigrettes

Salads in particular can highlight the vast range of ingredients treasured and revered by Indigenous communities from different locales. I've adapted these ten dishes from recipes originating from areas all across what is now the United States. It's truly a culinary journey—and I suspect you'll be deliciously surprised by at least one salad that's native to the place you live, or a place you love.

Most of these recipes are simple, fresh preparations that celebrate texture, seasonality, and the play of savory, smoky, and sweet. I generally serve my salads with light vinaigrettes to fully showcase their bounty of flavors—but the exception to that rule is my favorite of these recipes: a crunchy, creamy, sweet, succulent Dungeness crab salad with apples, walnuts, red pepper, and radicchio with a tangy yogurt-based dressing. Like any of my hearty and nutritious salads, it can be served as a starter or on its own.

Think about these recipes as ten ways to break out of your same-old-salad habit. The first, Amaranth with White Wine Vinaigrette (page 66), is the perfect illustration: there are no greens in it at all, just fresh bell peppers, scallions, and herbs alongside an earthy grain indigenous to South America that's still a staple food for Native Americans in what are now the southwestern states. Which isn't to say that traditionally, Native Americans didn't use fresh greens when they were available; they used them often, as additions to soups or cooked with vegetable or meat dishes. But the idea of eating a pile of cold, raw greens, in any season, topped with vegetables, meats, cheeses, and dressing is not a traditional Indigenous concept.

To suit modern tastes, I've created a few greens-heavy salads here—but of course even those incorporate the beans, nuts, and whole grains that would've been staple ingredients for Indigenous communities. They can also work as hearty sides to accompany the soups, roasted vegetables, or meat dishes elsewhere in this book.

As a bit of a challenge, I've included ingredients you may never have cooked with, or heard of, like cholla buds, foraged from cactus. I serve them with a lime vinaigrette to showcase the buds' essence of green bean and artichoke. And as a fervent hope, I've reminded you of dozens of ways to add crunch that are more flavorful, nutritious, and interesting than a crouton. Think pine nuts, watercress, fennel, jicama, swamp cabbage, pecans, and cranberries.

Eat your way through these salads, and before you're finished, you'll be seduced by the sprinkles of fresh sage, parsley, cilantro, and thyme. All my salads incorporate fresh herbs, which were, and still are, foraged by hundreds of Native American communities. You'll have a garden in your windowsill before you're through with this chapter: a little place to forage your own.

AMARANTH WITH WHITE WINE VINAIGRETTE

If you're unfamiliar with amaranth, think of it as a seed that tastes like a grain—similar in size, shape, and texture to quinoa. Amaranth has been cultivated for more than eight thousand years and was a staple food for the Aztecs and Indigenous communities of what's now the American Southwest. Unlike quinoa, it hasn't gained—or rather regained—widespread popularity, but I don't see this delicious secret being kept for very long. It has an earthy taste, most similar to brown rice or wheat berries; it's also rich in protein, vitamins, and minerals.

What I love most about cooking with amaranth is its versatility. It's gluten-free and can work in recipes including fruits, vegetables, greens, and other grains. It pairs especially well with squash, corn, cinnamon, sesame, and even chocolate. My trick in this flavorful recipe is to add a dash of vanilla to balance the earthiness and a sprinkling of a nice, light, acidic dressing to brighten the natural flavor but still keep it at the forefront. You can find amaranth fairly easily in health food stores or the grains section of the supermarket.

Serves 6 to 8

3 tablespoons canola oil

½ cup (75 g) diced yellow bell pepper

½ cup (50 g) diced celery

1 teaspoon vanilla extract

1 bay leaf

Salt and freshly cracked black pepper

4½ cups (1 L) chicken or vegetable stock

3 cups (600 g) dried amaranth

White Wine Vinaigrette, recipe follows

3 scallions, green part only, chopped, for garnish

In a medium pot over low heat, add the oil. When the oil is hot, add the bell pepper, celery, vanilla, bay leaf, and salt and pepper. Sweat the vegetables until soft, stirring occasionally, about 15 minutes. Increase the heat to high and add the stock. Bring to a boil. When boiling, add the amaranth and reduce the heat to low. Cover with a lid and let simmer for 25 minutes. At this point, all the stock should be absorbed. If any stock remains, use a fine-mesh strainer to remove the remaining liquid. Transfer the amaranth and vegetables to a serving bowl, remove the bay leaf, and add just enough white wine vinaigrette to lightly coat the salad, about ½ cup (120 ml). Try to avoid any vinaigrette pooling at the bottom of the bowl. Adjust the seasoning if necessary and garnish with scallions. This dish can be served hot, warm, or cold.

WHITE WINE VINAIGRETTE
Makes approximately 1 cup (240 ml)

¼ cup (60 ml) white wine vinegar

¾ cup (180 ml) olive oil

1 small shallot, peeled and minced

1 clove garlic, peeled and minced

1 teaspoon salt

1 teaspoon freshly cracked black pepper

In a small bowl, add the vinegar, oil, shallot, garlic, salt, and pepper. Whisk until well blended. Note: You may use a blender if you prefer. Reserve until ready to use. Any remaining dressing can be stored in an airtight container in the refrigerator for up to two weeks.

CHOLLA BUDS WITH PIÑON NUTS AND LIME VINAIGRETTE

In the high Sonoran Desert, there grows a native flowering cactus called cholla whose delectable buds taste similar to asparagus—with a hint of artichoke and a lemony twist. For thousands of years, the region's Indigenous people ate cholla buds in traditional dishes like this salad, though I've interwoven the familiar flavors of cucumber and cherry tomato to appeal to more contemporary tastes. I've dressed this offering with lime vinaigrette and incorporated texture and complexity with the addition of piñon nuts. Their bittersweet yet subtle flavor makes them a favorite ingredient in recipes of the Southwest. With the delightful combination of flavors presented in this salad, it's sure to be a crowd-pleaser. Note that if you'd like to make this dish, you'll need to plan at least a week ahead. Cholla buds can be difficult to find unless you're foraging in the deserts of Arizona, California, or Mexico. You can buy them dried from members of the Tohono O'odham Nation (see page 178), or you can purchase them fresh online. The wait will be worth it, I promise.

Serves 6 to 8

1 pound (455 g) Cooked Cholla Buds,
recipe follows

1 cup (125 g) diced red onion

2 cups (260 g) diced English cucumber

2 cups (290 g) yellow cherry tomatoes, halved

¼ cup (35 g) piñon nuts, toasted

Lime Vinaigrette, recipe follows

3 cups (120 g) loosely packed mixed greens

Salt and freshly cracked black pepper

¼ cup (30 g) crumbled queso fresco, for garnish

In a medium bowl, add the cooked cholla buds, onion, cucumber, tomatoes, and piñon nuts. Toss lightly with a little lime vinaigrette to coat. Add the mixed greens, gently toss again, and season with salt and pepper. Arrange on a serving platter and garnish with the queso fresco.

COOKED CHOLLA BUDS
Makes 1 pound (455 g)

2 cups (3.2 ounces/90 g) dried cholla buds

1 carrot, halved

1 stalk celery, halved

½ medium onion, peeled

1 tablespoon salt

1 tablespoon freshly cracked black pepper

In a large pot, add the cholla buds, carrot, celery, onion, 1 tablespoon salt, 1 tablespoon pepper, and 4 cups (960 ml) water or stock. Bring to a boil over high heat, then reduce the heat to low. Allow to simmer until the buds and vegetables are fork-tender, about 30 minutes. You may need to add more water if the liquid level gets low during the simmering process. When tender, remove the buds and arrange on a baking sheet to cool. The buds should have doubled in size. Discard the vegetables and liquid.

LIME VINAIGRETTE
Makes approximately ¾ cup (180 ml)

3 tablespoons lime juice

½ cup (120 ml) olive oil

1 tablespoon agave nectar

1 teaspoon salt

1 teaspoon freshly cracked black pepper

In a small bowl, add the lime juice, oil, agave nectar, 1 teaspoon salt, and 1 teaspoon pepper. Whisk until well combined. Reserve until ready to use.

CHOLLA BUDS WITH PIÑON NUTS
AND LIME VINAIGRETTE

Dried cholla buds, collected from cactus, taste like green beans crossed with asparagus and artichoke hearts.

This dish celebrates two distinctly Northwest favorites. I travel frequently to Washington State, and one thing I never miss while I'm there is the chance to eat fresh Dungeness crab. The meat is firm, delicate, light, and sweet—perfection, really. I'm including it here not only because I love it, but because there are dozens of Native American communities from Alaska and the Pacific Northwest who enjoy Dungeness crab in a variety of ways, including as a delightful addition to salads. If you live someplace where fresh crab is difficult to find, look for frozen. (Avoid imitation crab, since it won't provide the taste or texture you're looking for.) Washington is also known for apples. The best varieties for salads include the Pacific Rose, Pink Lady, Jazz, Honeycrisp, Granny Smith, Jonagold, and Gala. Go with whichever you like best. The dairy in this recipe is my addition; traditionally, Native Americans didn't keep domesticated animals that produced milk, so they didn't use dairy. But this sweet, tart, crunchy crab salad benefits from the cool creaminess of yogurt. If you'd like to skip the step of draining it through cheesecloth in a fine-mesh strainer overnight, use Greek yogurt in its place.

Serves 4

½ red apple, cored and diced

2 tablespoons lemon juice

1 pound (455 g) Dungeness crabmeat

1 shallot, peeled and minced

1 stalk celery, diced

½ red bell pepper, seeded and diced

3 tablespoons chopped walnuts

½ cup (120 ml) plain yogurt, drained

1 teaspoon salt

1 teaspoon freshly cracked black pepper

2 cups (80 g) chopped radicchio,
for garnish

In a medium bowl, toss the apple with the lemon juice—this will prevent the apple from oxidizing (turning brown). Then add the crab, shallot, celery, bell pepper, walnuts, yogurt, salt, and pepper. Stir well, but do not overmix. Arrange on a serving platter and garnish with the radicchio for a splash of color.

GREAT NORTHERN BEANS
WITH LEMON-THYME VINAIGRETTE

As you've probably gathered by now, beans are integral to Native American recipes. The previous chapter showed how versatile they can be in soups, and the same rule applies with salads. It wasn't common for ancient Native Americans to eat a lot of raw greens, but I think you'll appreciate that addition here, alongside the Great Northern beans that add to the play of colors: white beans in contrast to bright tomatoes, purple onions, green herbs, and vibrant lettuces. This dish is as pleasing to the eye as it is to the palate. The inclusion of protein-rich beans means that this salad can also work as a light and satisfying vegetarian lunch.

Serves 6 to 8

1 carrot, diced

1 stalk celery, diced

4½ cups (830 g) Great Northern beans, cooked (or two 15-ounce/425 g cans, drained and rinsed well)

2 cups (290 g) cherry tomatoes, halved

¾ cup (95 g) julienned red onion

½ cup (20 g) chopped fresh cilantro

4 cups (160 g) loosely packed mixed greens

Lemon-Thyme Vinaigrette, recipe follows

Salt and freshly cracked black pepper

In a medium bowl, add the carrot, celery, beans, tomatoes, onion, and cilantro. Stir well. Add the mixed greens and stir again. Toss the salad with a light coating of the lemon-thyme vinaigrette. Season to taste with salt and pepper and serve.

LEMON-THYME VINAIGRETTE
Makes approximately ¾ cup (180 ml)

3 tablespoons lemon juice

½ cup (120 ml) olive oil

2 teaspoons fresh thyme leaves, finely chopped

1 teaspoon salt

1 teaspoon freshly cracked black pepper

In a blender, add the lemon juice, oil, thyme, 1 teaspoon salt, and 1 teaspoon pepper. Puree until smooth. Reserve until ready to use. Any remaining dressing can be stored in an airtight container in the refrigerator for up to two weeks.

The Pequot and other New England communities have made variations of this hominy salad, and so have Cherokees from what are now the Carolinas. But my version came about by accident. One day, while lecturing at the College of the Holy Cross in Massachusetts, I did an impromptu cooking demonstration. A lecture guest happened to have brought some blue-corn hominy, so we made this easy, rustic salad with fresh herbs right there and then. I've added the bacon, but it's not necessary (or traditional); it's one of my favorite elements, though, since it adds flavor, richness, and texture. The pairing of salty bacon with tender hominy creates a comforting and hearty flavor combination while the infusion of lemon, parsley, and watercress adds a refreshing lightness. If you're not familiar with hominy, you're in for a treat with this salad; it's made from the kernels of dry corn, but with the tough outer hulls removed. It tastes a lot like popcorn but has the puffed, meaty feel of a chickpea. Best of all, it's easy to find and delicious straight from the can.

Serves 4 to 6

4 strips bacon, diced

4 cups (680 g) cooked hominy (canned is okay), rinsed well

¼ cup (35 g) diced onion (make sure dice is smaller than the hominy)

½ cup (75 g) diced red bell pepper

¼ cup (13 g) chopped fresh flat-leaf parsley

2 cloves garlic, peeled and minced

1 teaspoon ground sage

2 teaspoons salt

1 teaspoon freshly cracked black pepper

¼ cup (60 ml) olive oil

Zest and juice of 2 lemons

2 cups (70 g) loosely packed watercress

In a medium sauté pan, add the bacon and turn the heat to medium. Render the bacon until crispy, being careful not to let it burn. Remove the bacon bits and drain on a paper towel–lined plate. In a medium bowl, add the bacon bits, hominy, onion, bell pepper, parsley, garlic, sage, salt, and pepper. Stir well to combine. Stir in the oil, lemon zest, and lemon juice. Then stir in the watercress. Serve immediately.

MANOOMIN RICE FRITTER SALAD WITH BLUEBERRY VINAIGRETTE

I first made this salad, inspired by a Chippewa recipe, for Shane Plumer. Shane's Native name is Red Thunderbird, and he's a certified fitness trainer and yoga instructor who's been studying, practicing, and teaching therapeutic hatha yoga for more than a decade. We met through his work with Native communities and students across the nation, and one October, he invited me to be his guest at the White Earth Reservation—one of seven Chippewa reservations in north-central Minnesota (see page 124). There, we participated in a traditional wild rice harvest, which is just one of the ways

Shane's community honors its heritage and traditional foods. After we brought in that day's manoomin (a wild rice of the Native Americans, particularly communities of the Great Lakes) with our canoes, I made wild rice fritters for Shane and his family. There is nothing better than the aroma of fresh-cooked wild rice. I served the fritters with a fennel and blueberry salad—just as the ancient Chippewa would've done—but added a few personal touches: sweet red bell peppers and Parmesan. This wonderfully distinctive offering is a memorable treat that is sure to draw appreciation.

Serves 4 to 6

3 cups (270 g) julienned red bell pepper

2 cups (230 g) julienned carrots

½ cup (40 g) julienned fennel

Blueberry Vinaigrette, recipe follows

3 cups (120 g) loosely packed mixed greens

Manoomin Rice Fritters, recipe follows

1 cup (145 g) fresh blueberries

Freshly grated Parmesan cheese, as needed, optional

In a medium bowl, add the bell pepper, carrots, and fennel. Add ¼ cup (60 ml) of the blueberry vinaigrette and toss to combine. In a separate bowl, add the mixed greens and gently toss with 2 tablespoons of the blueberry vinaigrette. On a serving platter, arrange the dressed mixed greens, then top with the dressed vegetable mixture. Arrange the rice fritters on top and garnish with the blueberries and Parmesan (if using).

RECIPE CONTINUES

MANOOMIN RICE FRITTERS
Makes about 16 fritters

2 cups (290 g) Steamed Manoomin Rice
with Thyme (page 122)

3 tablespoons minced shallot

1 clove garlic, peeled and minced

¼ cup (35 g) chopped piñon nuts

¼ cup (40 g) frozen blueberries

¼ cup (30 g) all-purpose flour

2 egg whites

1 teaspoon salt

1 teaspoon freshly cracked black pepper

¼ cup (60 ml) canola oil

Prepare a paper towel–lined plate. In a bowl, add the rice, 3 tablespoons shallot, 1 clove garlic, piñon nuts, blueberries, flour, egg whites, 1 teaspoon salt, and 1 teaspoon pepper. Stir well to combine. Form patties using 2 tablespoons of the mixture for each patty. In a sauté pan over medium heat, add the canola oil.When the oil is hot, add the patties, making sure not to crowd the pan, cooking in batches if necessary. Sauté the fritters until golden brown, 2 to 3 minutes per side, then remove from the pan and set aside to cool on the prepared plate.

BLUEBERRY VINAIGRETTE
Makes approximately ¾ cup (180 ml)

2 tablespoons frozen blueberries

1 tablespoon agave nectar

Zest and juice of 1 lime

1 tablespoon diced shallot

1 clove garlic, peeled and minced

⅓ cup (75 ml) olive oil

1 teaspoon salt

1 teaspoon freshly cracked black pepper

In a blender, add the blueberries, agave nectar, lime zest and juice, 1 tablespoon shallot, and 1 clove garlic and blend. With the blender running, drizzle in the olive oil. Continue to blend until emulsified. Season with 1 teaspoon salt and 1 teaspoon pepper and reserve until ready to use. Any remaining dressing can be stored in an airtight container in the refrigerator for up to two weeks.

Fresh dandelion leaves are earthy and bitter; similar to radicchio in taste.

MANOOMIN RICE SALAD WITH APPLE-HONEY VINAIGRETTE

I recently took a trip to northern Minnesota to participate in a local rice harvest with the Ojibwe. Manoomin sprouts naturally in lakes and rivers there and is still harvested using traditional methods. My rice salad was inspired by that experience. Alongside members of the community, I paddled a canoe through the stalks and harvested the kernels by hand, using the same tools and methods the Ojibwe have used for thousands of years. This ancient, nutrient-rich wild rice translates into English as "harvesting berry" or "good berry," and it's still commonly found in Ojibwe recipes and ceremonies. Manoomin, like many traditional Native foods, is considered spiritual as well as sustaining. This recipe is intended to let you enjoy the elegant flavor of this ancient grain alongside crunchy nuts and watercress. I've added tart, sweet cranberries, as the Ojibwe would have—but I've also modernized it with a honey vinaigrette that gives this delightful salad just the right balance of earth, acid, and sweet.

Serves 4 to 6

4 cups (575 g) Steamed Manoomin Rice with Thyme (page 122), cooled

½ cup (55 g) shredded carrot

¼ cup (35 g) dried cranberries

½ cup (30 g) chopped scallions

½ cup (65 g) piñon nuts, toasted

Apple-Honey Vinaigrette, recipe follows

1 cup (35 g) loosely packed watercress

Salt and freshly cracked black pepper

In a medium bowl, add the rice, carrot, dried cranberries, scallions, and piñon nuts. Toss well and then drizzle with just enough apple-honey vinaigrette to coat the rice. Add the watercress, season with salt and pepper if necessary and toss again just before serving.

APPLE-HONEY VINAIGRETTE
Makes approximately ½ cup (120 ml)

2 tablespoons cider vinegar

1 tablespoon honey

6 tablespoons (90 ml) canola oil

Salt and freshly cracked black pepper

In a small bowl, add the vinegar and honey. Drizzle in the oil while whisking. Continue to whisk until emulsified. Season with salt and pepper and reserve until ready to use. Any remaining dressing can be stored in an airtight container in the refrigerator for up to two weeks.

MIXED GREENS AND DANDELION WITH JICAMA AND PRICKLY PEAR VINAIGRETTE

The prickly pear cactus began growing in the deserts of North America about three million years ago, so it's always appeared in recipes passed down from the Akimel O'odham and Tohono O'odham. In late August the deserts are accented with the cacti's rich, dark pink fruit, signaling that it's time to harvest. This recipe sticks with the delectable and time-honored tradition of combining fruits, nuts, and greens, but here, I'm updating the preparation of these ingredients by using raw greens and a zesty sprinkling of queso fresco to round out the flavors and bring some tart saltiness to the sweeter elements of the dish. Jicama and apples provide a refreshing crunch, while the star of this salad, for me, is the prickly pear vinaigrette, which highlights the fruit's unique flavor: a little like watermelon, a little like cranberry, with a fair amount of acid. It's the perfect complement to bitter or earthy greens like radicchio or the dandelion leaves this recipe calls for. If you can't find prickly pear juice or syrup in your grocery store, you can easily find it online. Just skip the agave if you're using syrup instead of juice—you don't want to over-sweeten the dressing.

Serves 6 to 8

2 cups (220 g) julienned green apple

2 tablespoons lemon juice

3 cups (385 g) julienned jicama

1 cup (110 g) julienned red onion

½ cup (60 g) chopped pecans

1 cup (40 g) loosely packed mixed greens

1 cup (55 g) chopped dandelion leaves

Prickly Pear Vinaigrette, recipe follows

2 teaspoons salt

2 teaspoons freshly cracked black pepper

½ cup (55 g) crumbled queso fresco

In a medium bowl, add the apple and lemon juice. Toss well, then add the jicama, onion, pecans, mixed greens, and dandelion leaves. Add just enough prickly pear vinaigrette to lightly coat the leaves. Season with 2 teaspoons salt and 2 teaspoons pepper and gently toss. Garnish with the queso fresco and serve.

PRICKLY PEAR VINAIGRETTE
Makes approximately ¾ cup (180 ml)

1 shallot, peeled and diced

2 cloves garlic, peeled and minced

Zest and juice of 1 lime

3 tablespoons prickly pear juice

1 tablespoon agave nectar

6 tablespoons (90 ml) olive oil

1 teaspoon salt

1 teaspoon freshly cracked black pepper

In a small bowl, add the shallot, garlic, lime zest and juice, prickly pear juice, and agave nectar. Drizzle in the oil while whisking. Continue to whisk until emulsified. Stir in 1 teaspoon salt and 1 teaspoon pepper and reserve until ready to use. Any remaining dressing can be stored in an airtight container in the refrigerator for up to two weeks.

SWAMP CABBAGE SALAD WITH LEMON VINAIGRETTE

I think of this salad as a celebration of springtime and the first green leaves of the season—a signal that variety and abundance are nearing after a long winter of heartier fare. This salad is inspired by a Seminole recipe and features hearts of palm, which they'd have called swamp cabbage, foraged from the cabbage palm that grows wild in what's now Florida. Swamp cabbage is often canned and available at most grocery stores, and it's perfect in a salad: light, healthy, mild enough to pair with all kinds of vegetables, but with a signature nutty, creamy, vegetal flavor somewhere in the overlap of water chestnut and artichoke. Swamp cabbage is the ideal opposite of the sweet spice of red pepper and cool crispness of cucumber I've added to the traditional salad, and it pairs equally well with candied nuts and raw onion. This salad is hearty enough to serve as a main course—and while I use a mixture of field greens to add shape, texture, and color, you can adjust for what's in season, or use whichever baby lettuce you prefer: arugula, butter, dandelion, frisée, or spinach. This delightful salad with just enough Lemon Vinaigrette to coat the greens is healthy, delicious, and sure to please.

Serves 4 to 6

Mixed field greens, as needed, washed

1 pound (455 g) hearts of palm, cleaned and sliced into coins

1 red bell pepper, seeded and julienned

1 English cucumber, peeled and sliced

½ red onion, peeled and thinly sliced

¼ cup (25 g) candied pecans

Lemon Vinaigrette, recipe follows

In a large serving bowl, add the mixed greens, hearts of palm, bell pepper, cucumber, onion, and pecans. Toss well and drizzle with just enough lemon vinaigrette to coat the salad.

LEMON VINAIGRETTE
Makes approximately ¼ cup (60 ml)

Zest of 1 lemon

2 teaspoons lemon juice

1 small shallot, peeled and diced

1 clove garlic, peeled and minced

Salt and freshly cracked black pepper

2 tablespoons canola oil

In a small bowl, add the lemon zest and juice, shallot, garlic, and salt and pepper. Whisk together, then slowly drizzle in the oil while continuing to whisk. Reserve until ready to use. Any remaining dressing can be stored in an airtight container in the refrigerator for up to two weeks.

Seminoles and Muscogee

The Seminoles and Muscogee (Miccosukee) are two Indigenous communities composed of many different bands in what is now Florida, as well as regions further north. The Seminole community of Florida was formed as an organization in 1957 for a declaration of tribal sovereignty. In 1962, the Miccosukee community of Florida was formed to enable them to make more specialized policies. The name *Seminole* includes a diverse region of different ancestral communities united. The origin of the name comes from the Muscogee word *simanó-li*, which was adopted as *cimarrón* by the Spanish, meaning "runaway" or "wild one."

I love traditional Seminole architecture, seamlessly adapted to the state's humidity and local resources. Supported by strong cypress log frames with lovely sleeping quarters upstairs, the homes, called chickees, are protected by palmetto thatch roofs to repel heavy rainstorms. With their beautiful textured thatch roofs, chickees remain a popular feature today for tourist resorts in Florida. You can even hire Native American architects to design and build one for you.

This architecture is just one of the ways palms are central to Indigenous culture. Palmetto thatch protects homes by repelling the elements, and hearts of palm are a staple of the Native American diet. Traditionally, communities like the Seminoles ate when they were hungry and didn't have a regimented meal schedule. Relaxed snacking throughout the day, whenever feeling peckish, is another Seminole way. Culinarily speaking, both the Seminoles and Muscogee are best known for their sofkee—a slightly sour rice or corn porridge, the kind of taste you'd get from adding yogurt to your oatmeal or granola. Soup or sofkee traditionally was kept warm, the way some people like to keep their rice cooker on "warm mode" throughout the day. It's a convenient way to keep everyone well fed and happy when on different schedules.

TRADITIONALLY, COMMUNITIES LIKE THE SEMINOLES ATE WHEN THEY WERE HUNGRY AND DIDN'T HAVE A REGIMENTED MEAL SCHEDULE.

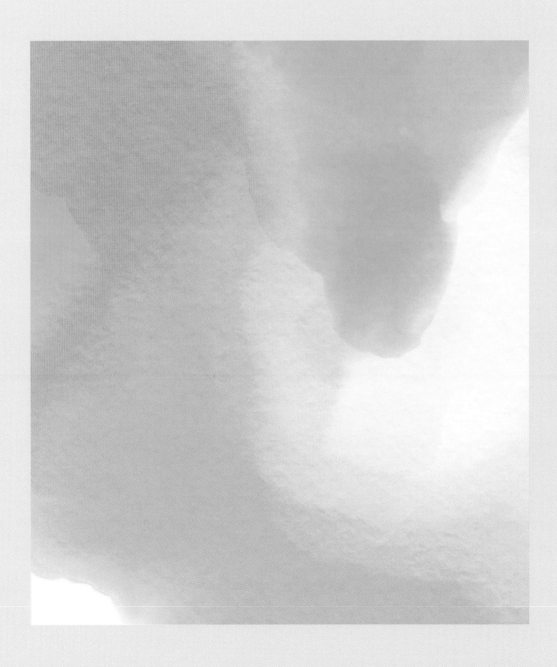

THREE SISTERS SALAD WITH SHALLOT VINAIGRETTE

I can't attribute this simple summer recipe to any particular community; rather, it's a gesture of gratitude for seasonal bounties and the three sisters—corn, squash, and beans—at the heart of so many Native American recipes. This salad, with its savory shallot vinaigrette, will be a true celebration if your herbs and veggies come straight from the garden or farm stand.

Serves 6 to 8

1 tablespoon canola oil

1 small onion, peeled and diced

2 cloves garlic, peeled and minced

1 carrot, diced

1 stalk celery, diced

3 sprigs fresh thyme

1 bay leaf

Salt and freshly cracked black pepper

1½ cups (175 g) squash or zucchini, cut into small cubes

1½ cups (220 g) fresh corn kernels

1½ cups (270 g) cooked and rinsed white beans

3 cups (60 g) spinach leaves

Shallot Vinaigrette, recipe follows

In a large sauté pan over medium heat, add the canola oil. When the oil is hot, add the onion, 2 cloves garlic, carrot, celery, thyme, and bay leaf. Sweat the vegetables until soft, about 10 minutes, stirring occasionally. Season with a pinch of salt and pepper. Add the squash and corn and cook until fork-tender, about 10 minutes. Add the beans and spinach and allow to warm, stirring occasionally. Remove from the heat and transfer to a serving bowl. Discard the bay leaf and thyme sprigs and toss the salad with just enough shallot vinaigrette to coat. Serve warm or at room temperature.

SHALLOT VINAIGRETTE
Makes approximately ⅓ cup (75 ml)

1 tablespoon lemon juice

1 shallot, peeled and minced

1 clove garlic, peeled and minced

¼ cup (60 ml) olive oil

Salt and freshly cracked black pepper

In a small bowl, add the lemon juice, shallot, and 1 clove garlic. Drizzle in the olive oil while whisking. Continue to whisk until emulsified. Season with salt and pepper and reserve until ready to use. Any remaining dressing can be stored in an airtight container in the refrigerator for up to two weeks.

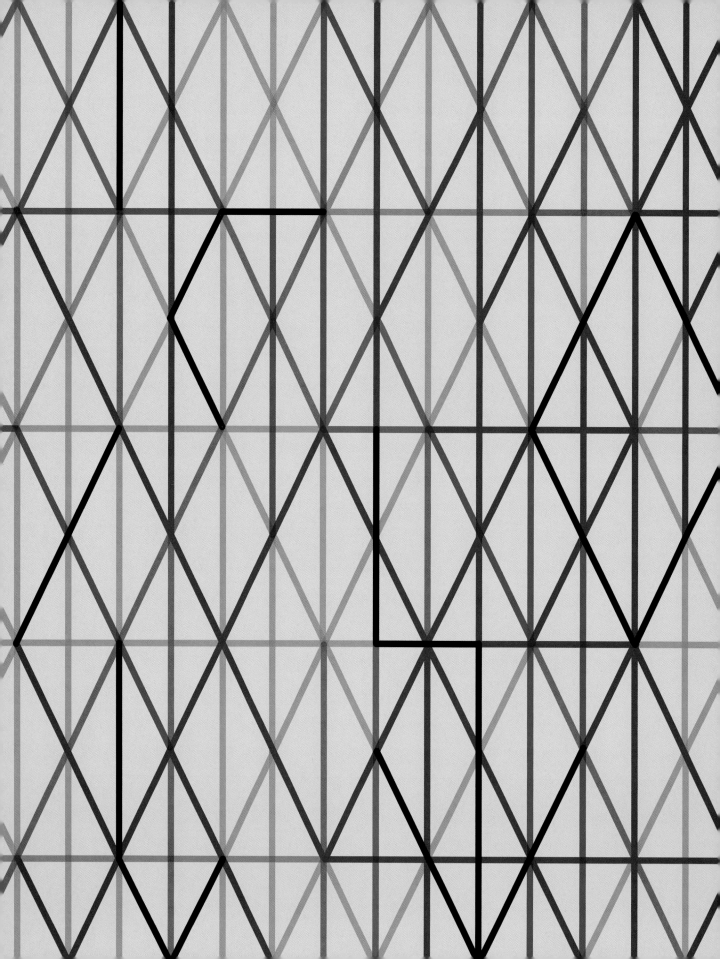

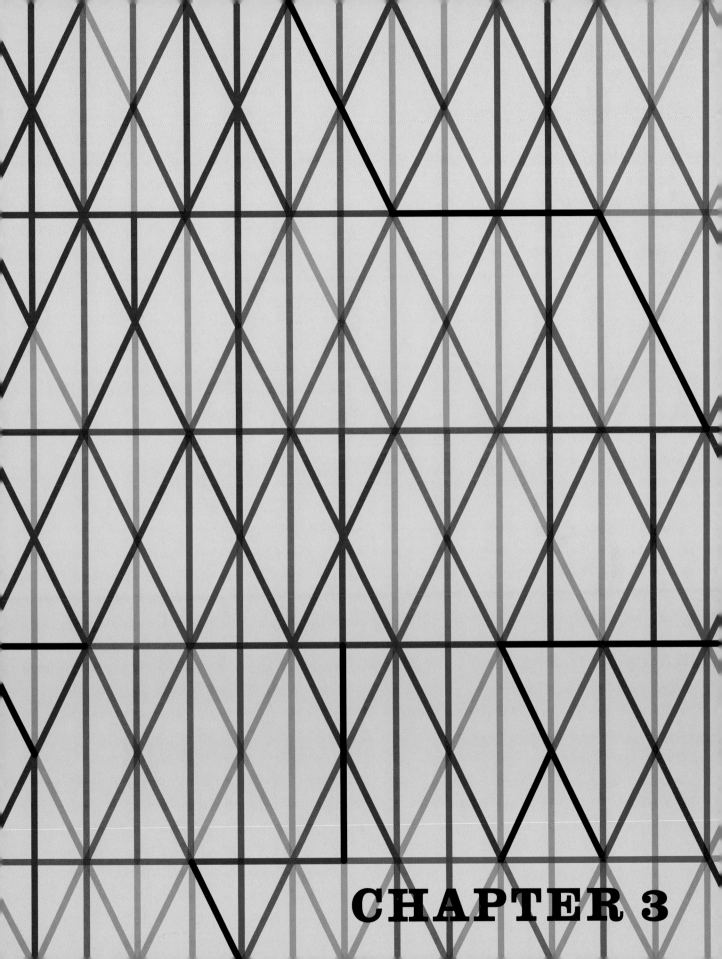

CHAPTER 3

Vegetables and Starches

It's impossible to talk about Native American food traditions without talking about nature, the ever-changing seasons, and the spiritual relationship between Indigenous people and the foods that sustain us. Many of our most deeply held beliefs exist around planting, growing, harvesting, and cooking—honoring plant and animal spirits and giving back to the earth that gives to us.

This chapter's recipes focus on what grows wild and what can be harvested locally and in season, but even more than that, they celebrate the ancient Native American culinary tradition of creativity. If you've ever been bored by the handful of vegetables and starches you're always eating—particularly in winter, when fresh-picked items are limited—prepare to be newly inspired.

True, traditional Native American recipes depend heavily on root vegetables, wild rice, and the three sisters of corn, beans, and squash, but they also burst with fresh produce and foraged foods from forests, deserts, plains, lakes, and rivers. The staple foods featured in this chapter's dishes are some of the oldest on earth, and yet they never get old.

Corn goes back ten thousand years, and squash goes back eight thousand, so it makes sense that squash blossoms, seeds, and flesh have been incorporated into countless traditional dishes and that corn has been used in every imaginable recipe, including one called pemmican, which I think of as one of the first-known protein energy bars. Likewise, I've tried to honor what's ancient and celebrate what's new in every changing season.

Summer squash is sometimes mashed, other times sliced and sautéed or served alongside fresh tomatoes, bell peppers, onions, and herbs. Fall and winter squash is baked with agave, walnuts, and cranberry, or grilled with foraged herbs and natural sweeteners. Spring brings wilted greens and bright fern fiddleheads. Summer beans are stewed with vine-ripe tomatoes or tossed with just-picked vegetables;

in fall and winter they're mashed by hand, along the lines of mashed potatoes. Wild rice in summer pairs with colorful squash and lemony herbs; in winter it tastes of piñon nuts and cranberry. Wintry root vegetables can be sweet—glazed and caramelized—or savory—mashed or pureed. Corn is for every season, with its kernels served fresh or ground into savory meal that'll rival any Italian polenta; and desert landscapes carry nopales, or cactus paddles, to the kitchen all year round as well.

These cycles turn and turn, but the ancient foods never feel tired: savor these vibrant, versatile, nourishing vegetables and starches with the seasonal salads, soups, and meat dishes in this book. Consider their ancient histories and welcome the abiding spirit they bring to your table.

BAKED FARMER GOURDS

When I was a boy living in New Mexico, I loved helping my grandmother tend to her garden. She grew melons and several varieties of squash. Every fall, there'd be an abundance of gourds, which she turned into hearty, autumnal side dishes like this one. We must've eaten squash two or three times a week back then, lightly sweetened. In this recipe, I use agave as a sweetener; my grandmother used brown sugar; and for centuries before honeybees were imported, Native communities used maple sugar. If you don't have agave on hand, brown sugar or maple syrup are easy substitutes—just use a light touch so you're enhancing, not smothering, the squash's natural essence. You'll love the play of textures as well as flavors in this dish, something simple made special with the earthy crunch of walnuts, soft sweetness of squash, and the juniper berries' slight hint of pine.

Serves 4 to 6

1 acorn squash, peeled, seeded, and diced

1 cup (115 g) diced peeled butternut squash

1 cup (115 g) diced peeled kabocha squash

½ cup (50 g) walnuts

3 juniper berries, ground

½ cup (120 ml) agave nectar

¼ cup (60 ml) canola oil

2 teaspoons salt

2 teaspoons freshly cracked black pepper

¼ cup (13 g) chopped fresh flat-leaf parsley

Preheat the oven to 350°F (175°C).

In a medium bowl, add the acorn, butternut, and kabocha squashes along with the walnuts, juniper berries, agave nectar, and oil. Toss well to combine. Season with the salt and pepper.

Line a baking sheet with parchment paper. Arrange the squash mixture on the pan. Place in the oven and bake for 30 to 40 minutes, or until the squashes are fork-tender. Remove from the oven and transfer to a serving platter. Garnish with the parsley before serving.

BLUE CORNMEAL

During a filming of one of her shows, Lidia Bastianich, Emmy Award–winning television host and bestselling cookbook author, turned to me and said, "It's the Italians who found the niche with ground corn dishes." After a pause, I smiled and said, "I'm sorry, Lidia, but I believe it was the Native Americans." I showed her this blue cornmeal recipe, which is similar to the creamy polenta you'll see in Italian recipes. But there are a few important differences: I use meal from blue corn, also known as Hopi maize.

It's the same ingredient Native Americans used for thousands of years in what's now Mexico and the American Southwest. I make my traditional cornmeal with pride and pleasure, and I think you'll also appreciate the sweet, full corn flavor as well as the beautiful violet color. Cook with homemade stock if you have it; you can always taste the difference. And for a truly authentic version, make it without the cheese—but I love the addition of salty, tangy queso fresco.

Serves 6 to 8

4 cups (960 ml) chicken or vegetable stock

1 cup (120 g) blue cornmeal

1 tablespoon salt

1 tablespoon freshly cracked black pepper

Paprika, for garnish, optional

¼ cup (15 g) chopped scallions, green part only

In a large, heavy-bottom pot, add the stock and bring to a boil over high heat. When boiling, slowly add the cornmeal while stirring. Add the salt and pepper. Stir constantly while keeping an eye on the cornmeal (it will burn if not attended to). The cornmeal is ready when it thickens and pulls away from the sides of the pot, 5 to 7 minutes. Remove from the heat and adjust the seasoning if necessary. Garnish with paprika, if using, and scallions and serve immediately.

CALABASAS SQUASH, TOMATOES, AND QUESO FRESCO

For the Indigenous people of the Western Hemisphere, squash has always been an important food source. It's believed to be the oldest cultivated food in North America, but that's just one of the reasons I give it so much attention in these recipes. Besides its historical significance, squash is versatile and delicious. This dish is named for what's now Calabasas, California, originally home to the Chumash. They lived among the hills and canyons, relying on wildlife for sustenance as well as the fruits and vegetables that grew easily in the region's rich soil. This dish reflects the foods native to that area, and my recipe can work with any summer squash. I especially like pattypan, which is denser and crunchier than other summer varieties. Yellow squash works well, and so does common green zucchini—though I prefer golden zucchini for its more delicate, sweeter taste. Keep this recipe handy in late summer and early autumn when summer squash is plentiful, tomatoes are at their peak, and bell peppers and chilies are just-picked—you'll taste the entire season in every bite.

Serves 6 to 8

2 tablespoons canola oil

¼ cup (35 g) diced yellow onion

1 cup (145 g) fresh corn kernels

½ cup (75 g) chopped green chilies

1 cup (150 g) chopped green bell pepper

1 pound (455 g) thinly sliced summer squash

1 vine-ripe tomato, diced

Salt and freshly cracked black pepper

¼ cup (30 g) crumbled queso fresco

¼ cup (13 g) chopped fresh flat-leaf parsley

In a large sauté pan over medium-low heat, add the oil. When the oil is hot, add the onion and sauté just until the onion begins to soften. Add the corn, green chilies, and bell pepper and sauté for 5 minutes. Next, add the squash and tomato and sauté for another 5 minutes. Season with salt and pepper and stir. Cover the pan with a lid and cook until the squash is tender, about 10 minutes. Sprinkle with the queso fresco and parsley just before serving.

Chumash

With ancestral lands in southern, central, and coastal California, Chumash territory spans from what is now Malibu to San Luis Obispo. The name *Malibu* in Chumash means "the surf sounds lovely." If you've ever seen the stars over the ocean of California's coast, it's easy to understand how the Chumash became talented astronomers who accurately mapped constellations, some of which were recorded as arborglyphs—like petroglyphs but carved into trees.

Arborglyphs can be found on trees in the Chumash and Yokut regions of California's central coast. Some of the carvings look like angular lizards, used as sundials to track the movement of shadow over the seasons. Using this astronomy tool like a calendar, the ancient Chumash knew when solstices and equinoxes were coming. This helped determine planting seasons and is a lot more accurate than modern calendars that have to add or take away extra days for leap years.

The Chumash's reverence for the cosmos is also evident in their political structures. Alchuklash, scholarly civic leaders, taught astronomy and emphasized the connection between the sky and earth. As political advisors, teachers, and scientists, their role was to guide the well-being of the community.

Alchuklash storytellers explained the winter solstice with a tale about Sky Coyote and Old Man Sun playing a gambling game called peon. If Old Man Sun wins the game by guessing correctly where Sky Coyote has hidden his bone, then he can retire from his job of warming the earth. Festivals and celebrations still exist where Chumash play the human version of the peon game, in which they sing, chant, and share traditional foods.

California has always been known for its luscious crops and growing seasons, and Chumash recipes reflect this. Their traditional recipes are a bounty of fish and mussels, as well as geese and rabbits, which were traditionally hunted with a stick similar to a boomerang. Their salads feature clover, a bright fresh accompaniment to the nuttiness of acorn pancakes.

However, this abundance of food the Chumash depend on isn't always guaranteed. Entering into a new year is always fraught with hope and anxiety. Will the year bring good things? For the Chumash, this precipice of uncertainty in the new year is a time for reflection and planning. It's also a time for the Alchuklash to remind people that the universe is holistically connected; one can feel confident that the seasons will move through time just as the shadows of the lizard move across arborglyph trees.

CALIFORNIA HAS ALWAYS BEEN KNOWN FOR ITS LUSCIOUS CROPS AND
GROWING SEASONS, AND CHUMASH RECIPES REFLECT THIS.

GLAZED ROOT VEGETABLES

I first learned to forage from my grandmother, who'd take me into the forests of Colorado on weekends and show me where to find piñon nuts, wild onions, and root vegetables like carrots, parsnips, and sunchokes. After filling our baskets, we'd return home and braise the vegetables to perfection—it's a technique nearly as easy as roasting, but even more delicious. Since then, I've perfected my root vegetable recipes, getting creative while staying (mostly) true to the traditions of the Hopi, Zuni, Ute, Navajo, and White Mountain Apache communities (see pages 56, 134, 146, 200, and 208) of the Colorado Plateau, where these vegetables have always grown wild. Make substitutions based on what you like; any root vegetables will work, as long as you cut them the same size so they cook evenly. But try not to skip the fennel; the slight hint of anise really adds to the glaze—as does the splash of white wine, though that's obviously not a traditional ingredient. No need to peel your root vegetables; you'll lose nutritional value, and the earthy flavor is intended to complement the caramelization of the vegetables. Sear them well so they'll release their natural sugars; that's the secret to this simple, delectable, autumnal dish.

Serves 4 to 6

2 tablespoons canola oil

2 fennel bulbs, cleaned, leafy tops removed, and the bulb cut into wedges

3 carrots, unpeeled and cut to the length of the fennel bulbs, then halved

1 medium turnip, cleaned and diced

1 medium onion, peeled and cut into wedges

½ cup (120 ml) dry white wine

2 cups (480 ml) vegetable or chicken stock

2 teaspoons salt

2 teaspoons freshly cracked black pepper

2 tablespoons chopped fresh flat-leaf parsley, for garnish

Preheat the oven to 350°F (175°C).

In a large, heavy-bottom sauté pan over high heat, add the oil and heat, but don't let the oil smoke. When the oil is hot, add some of the fennel, carrots, turnip, and onion. Note: You will likely need to cook in batches. Sear the vegetables until they have a nice caramelized crust. Remove from the pan and continue with the next batch. When finished searing, add all the seared vegetables back to the pan. Add the wine to deglaze, scraping up any browned bits stuck to the bottom of the pan, and allow all the wine to be completely cooked out. Next, add the stock and bring to a boil. Once boiling, cover the pan and transfer to the oven and braise for 30 minutes, or until the vegetables are fork-tender. Remove from the oven, stir in the salt and pepper, and serve warm with a sprinkling of chopped parsley on top.

GRILLED BUTTERNUT SQUASH

Butternut squash is a fairly common ingredient these days, and that's something I'm happy to see. Inside their tan-yellow skin (which you always need to peel) is a sweet and nutty pale orange flesh that's sweeter than pumpkin, with a more delicate texture. Butternuts are considered a winter squash but they can stay fresh for months—which is why I almost always have one lying around on my kitchen counter. It's also why many Native communities, including the Haudenosaunee who lived in what's now New York State, considered them a year-round staple. They'd often roast butternuts directly over a fire, so this recipe works in the spirit of that tradition, trading a grill for an open fire. If you like squash roasted, you'll love it grilled too. Fresh sage, shallots, and agave instantly elevate this recipe, turning a "there's-nothing-in-the-fridge" moment into a hearty, crowd-pleasing side dish.

Serves 4 to 6

¼ cup (60 ml) canola oil

1 tablespoon agave nectar

1 teaspoon salt

1 teaspoon freshly cracked black pepper

½ shallot, peeled, seeded, and diced

1 tablespoon chopped fresh sage leaves

1 butternut squash, peeled, seeded, and cut into ¼-inch (6 mm) slices

In a medium bowl, add the oil, agave nectar, salt, pepper, shallot, and sage. Stir well. Add the squash to the bowl and stir to coat. Heat a grill pan over high heat. When the pan is hot, grill the squash for about 3 minutes on each side. Remove from the heat, adjust the seasoning if necessary, and serve warm.

GRILLED CACTUS PADDLES

Cactus paddles have always been considered a delicacy in Native American cuisine, particularly by the Navajo of what's now southern Arizona. All cacti are edible, but nopales are some of the best—especially tasty served hot, directly off the grill, as a side to accompany a cold summer salad and/or grilled meats, fruits, and vegetables. You'll have to try them to really understand their flavor, but if you can imagine a vegetable somewhere in between a green bean, bell pepper, and okra—with a hint of tart, slightly bitter citrus—you'll get the idea. Most modern recipes will instruct you to salt, drain, rinse, and rub the cactus paddles to remove the slime that's part of their essence—but Native American recipes welcome and incorporate the natural liquid. If you'd prefer to avoid it, remove the nopales from the heat when they're still a bit firm; overcooking releases more liquid. When you're choosing cactus paddles, feel for tenderness and a slight give—the same way you'd choose an avocado. Look for paddles a little larger than your hand. And I can't stress this enough: be careful when removing the spines. I speak from experience. When I was around age thirteen, out picking piñons with my family, my brother thought it would be funny to yell "Snake!" I turned and ran, tripped, and fell right into a cactus. Despite the still-fresh memory of the sting of those spines in my hands and arms, I still love cactus. But as a food, not a houseplant: to the Navajo, cactus is sacred and should flourish in the wild.

Serves 6 to 8

6 cactus paddles, cleaned (see page 110)

2 teaspoons canola oil

1 teaspoon salt

1 teaspoon freshly cracked black pepper

In a large bowl or casserole dish, add the cactus paddles, oil, salt, and pepper. Toss well and allow to marinate while preparing an outdoor grill to high heat. When the grill reaches temperature, arrange the cactus paddles on the grill and grill each side for about 4 minutes. Remove from the heat and thinly slice. Adjust the seasoning if necessary and serve immediately.

Cleaning Cactus Paddles

Before you can make Indigenous dishes using cactus paddles, or nopales, you first must remove the spines. Here's how you do it.

Step One

Begin by placing the paddle, or nopal, on a large cutting board. Hold it in place with your fingers in an area where there aren't any spines, or use tongs or a towel—whatever you're comfortable with. Next, with a sharp knife, carefully slice a thin layer around the outer edge of the nopal, which will remove the outer spines.

Step Two

With a knife or vegetable peeler, slowly and carefully remove the spines on both flat surfaces of the nopal by slicing and scraping. The key here is to take your time.

Step Three

Once all the spines are removed, gently rinse the nopal under running water and wipe dry with paper towels or a clean kitchen towel. You can now use the nopal or store it for later use. To store, simply place in a zip-top bag and keep in the refrigerator for no more than a week.

MANOOMIN RICE CAKES

Wild rice cakes are common in Native American cuisine (a more customary preparation can be found on page 80), but these use wheat flour, which isn't traditional at all. I love how the crispy breading holds the still-crunchy vegetables and wild rice inside; it also lends a little more structure to the cakes, which tend to fall apart if you substitute cornmeal. The best part about these rice cakes is that they're scrumptious warm or cold, by themselves or as a side dish, for breakfast, lunch, or dinner. I especially like to serve them warm, as an appetizer.

Serves 6 to 8

For the rice cakes:

6 cups (865 g) Steamed Manoomin Rice with Thyme (page 122)

1 shallot, peeled and diced

¼ cup (25 g) diced red bell pepper

¼ cup (25 g) diced yellow bell pepper

¼ cup (30 g) diced and sautéed zucchini

½ cup (25 g) chopped fresh flat-leaf parsley

2 eggs, beaten

¼ cup (60 ml) canola oil

1 tablespoon salt

1 tablespoon freshly cracked black pepper

Fresh parsley, for garnish, optional

Chipotle Aioli, optional, recipe follows

For the breading and frying:

2 cups (250 g) all-purpose flour

1 teaspoon salt

1 teaspoon freshly cracked black pepper

2 eggs, beaten

2 cups (200 g) fine bread crumbs

¼ cup (60 ml) canola oil

For the chipotle aioli:

6 chipotle chilies in adobo sauce

1 cup (240 ml) mayonnaise

2 teaspoons lemon or lime juice

¼ teaspoon salt

¼ teaspoon freshly ground black pepper

Make the rice cakes: In a food processor, add the rice and pulse a few times to roughly chop it. Do not overprocess, as the rice should be coarse, not fine. Remove the rice and transfer to a large bowl. Add the shallot, bell peppers, zucchini, parsley, eggs, oil, salt, and pepper. Stir well to combine. Scoop 3 tablespoons (40 g) of the rice mixture at a time and, using your fingers, form into cakes (about 4 per serving).

Make the breading: In a medium bowl, combine the flour, salt, and pepper. In a separate medium bowl, add the beaten eggs. In a third medium bowl, add the bread crumbs. Preheat the oven to 350°F (175°C). In a large sauté pan over high heat, add the oil. Dredge the rice cakes first in the flour mixture, shaking off excess, then in the egg wash, and then in the bread crumbs, shaking off excess. Cooking in batches, place each breaded cake into the hot oil and sear each side until golden brown. Remove the cakes from the oil and transfer them to a baking sheet. Bake for 25 to 35 minutes, or until cooked through. Remove from the oven, garnish with fresh parsley (if using), and serve with a side of chipotle aioli, if desired.

Make the chipotle aioli: In a food processor, add the chilies with a little of the adobo sauce. Puree to a paste. Transfer to a small bowl and set aside. In a small bowl, whisk together the mayonnaise, lemon or lime juice, and salt and pepper. Add a little of the pureed chilies to the bowl and whisk until combined. Taste, and if necessary add more of the pureed chilies until the aioli reaches your desired spice level. Transfer the aioli to an airtight container and store in the refrigerator until ready to use, for up to a week.

MASHED CRANBERRY BEANS WITH COCONUT MILK

If you haven't tried cranberry beans, look for their long, bright pink pods in late summer and fall when they're abundant at farmers' markets, ready to be shucked. They might be the most beautiful of all the beans: small, white, and flecked with deep cranberry-red patterns. While their appearance is part of the pleasure of cooking with them, there are practical reasons too. They're nutty, sweet, and meaty, and their delicate skin makes them perfect for mashing. It's common in Native American recipes to mash beans with a fork so their fluffy insides create an entirely different texture and their flavors really bloom. I've taken that mashing technique even further here, adding coconut milk to create a light, nutty creaminess. It's also a celebration of another Indigenous staple: cranberries. This recipe is close to perfect without them, but I absolutely love the bright color and tart flavor of the cranberries among the mashed beans.

Serves 6 to 8

3 tablespoons canola oil

1 small onion, peeled and diced

1 clove garlic, peeled and minced

1 tablespoon salt

1 tablespoon freshly cracked black pepper

¼ cup (25 g) fresh or frozen cranberries

4 cups (710 g) cooked cranberry beans

½ cup (120 ml) coconut milk

In a heavy-bottom pan over medium heat, add the oil. When the oil is hot, add the onion, garlic, salt, pepper, and cranberries. Sauté, stirring occasionally, until the onions and cranberries are soft, about 15 minutes. Add the beans and cook until heated through. Remove from the heat and, using a food mill or potato ricer, mash the bean mixture. Return the mashed beans to the pan. Over medium heat, stir in the coconut milk. Adjust the seasoning if necessary and stir until a mashed potato consistency is achieved. Serve immediately.

SAUTÉED ACORN SQUASH
WITH MAPLE SYRUP

I came up with this recipe while visiting the James Bay Market in Victoria, British Columbia. I'd been invited to prepare a dinner that evening to celebrate the First Nations of what's now Canada. Squash and maple syrup were already on my mind, given the region's traditional Indigenous cuisine. But to round out the sweet-on-sweet flavor profile, I added the crunchy, mild spice of green bell pepper. Piñon nuts add a sprinkle of buttery, nutty goodness, and you have a dish that's hearty enough to be its own lunch or brunch, or—as I served it—a side to accompany meat dishes and seasonal vegetables.

Serves 4 to 6

¼ cup (60 ml) canola oil

2 acorn squash, peeled, seeded, and sliced

1 cup (125 g) sliced red onion

¼ cup (25 g) sliced green bell pepper

1 clove garlic, peeled and minced

¼ cup (35 g) chopped piñon nuts

¼ cup (60 ml) maple syrup

1 teaspoon salt

1 teaspoon freshly cracked black pepper

¼ cup (15 g) chopped scallions,
green part only

In a large sauté pan over high heat, add the oil. When the oil is hot, add the squash, onion, and bell pepper and sauté while stirring to sear and soften the vegetables, about 3 minutes. Add the garlic and piñon nuts and continue to sauté and stir for another 8 minutes, or until the squash is soft and golden brown. Note: You're cooking at high heat, so it's important to keep the vegetables moving so they don't burn. Stir in the maple syrup and remove from the heat. Season with the salt and pepper and garnish with the scallions just before serving.

SAUTÉED FIDDLEHEADS
WITH APPLE

Fiddleheads are the curled fronds of young ferns that grow wild in the damp shady areas of lowland forests in spring. They appear often in recipes passed down from Indigenous communities of what's now northeast America and southeast Canada; they're delicious, with a vegetal flavor along the lines of asparagus and baby spinach and the texture of a green bean. Find fiddleheads at farmers' markets or gourmet grocery stores during their short spring season. To soften them a bit but keep their fresh firmness intact, I like to blanch fiddleheads before tossing them into salads and sides like this one, where the grassiness of sautéed fiddleheads plays off the sugary, tart crispness of apple. McIntosh are the most authentic apples for this recipe, but choose whatever variety you like best. I always think about color and texture, though—bright red or pink to accent the green, and an apple that's all at once crunchy, sweet, and tart. A little shallot and lemon brighten the earthiness of the ferns and round out this beautiful, delectable, fresh seasonal side dish.

Serves 4 to 6

¼ cup (45 g) diced red apple

1 tablespoon lemon juice

3 tablespoons canola oil

1 pound (455 g) fiddleheads, blanched (see page 120)

¼ cup (35 g) diced shallot

1 small clove garlic, peeled and minced

1 teaspoon salt

1 teaspoon freshly cracked black pepper

In a small bowl, add the apple and lemon juice. Stir well and set aside.

In a large sauté pan over high heat, add the oil. When the oil is hot, add the fiddleheads, shallot, and garlic. Sauté for 6 to 7 minutes, stirring constantly so the vegetables don't burn. Add the apple and continue to sauté with the fiddleheads for 1 minute. Stir in the salt and pepper. Remove from the heat, adjust the seasoning if necessary and serve immediately.

Blanching Fiddlehead Ferns

Blanching is a basic French technique. It's a quick two-step process in which a vegetable is briefly boiled and then plunged into an ice-water bath to immediately stop the cooking process while still ensuring the vegetable is bright and tender-crisp. Because fiddleheads are known to carry foodborne illness, always make sure to cook them further after blanching, and do not eat them raw.

Step One

Make sure the fiddleheads are trimmed and cleaned.

Step Two

Fill a pot large enough to hold the fiddleheads with water and season with a good fist of salt. Bring to a rolling boil over high heat. While waiting for the water to boil, fill a bowl with cold water and lots of ice. Blanch the fiddleheads in the boiling water for about 2 minutes, or until the water returns to a boil. You can also blanch in batches.

Step Three

Quickly remove the fiddleheads from the boiling water using a slotted spoon and immediately plunge them into the ice-water bath. This process is called shocking—it immediately stops the cooking process, allowing the enzymes in the vegetable to keep its color and crispness.

Step Four

Once the fiddleheads are ice cold, remove them from the water and pat them dry with paper towels; now they're ready to be sautéed or cooked further using another method. You can also place the fiddleheads in freezer bags at this stage and freeze for use later.

STEAMED MANOOMIN RICE
WITH THYME

Some species of wild rice date back more than twelve thousand years—so it was, is, and always will be an important staple in Native American cuisine. To enjoy it the way it's meant to taste, avoid paddy-grown, machine-harvested wild rice; you can recognize it from its almost-black, very hard kernels, which lack the rich, fragrant nuttiness of rice that grows naturally in rivers and lakes. Authentic manoomin has rough, uneven, medium-brown kernels; it's also fluffier, more tender and flavorful. In the case of this recipe, it's the rice itself that's worth celebrating. Make it even more delicious with garden-fresh herbs and homemade stock. This time-honored recipe will complement virtually any meal in this book—or any of your well-known favorites. Substitute any fresh herb to create different flavor profiles or to use whatever's in season.

Serves 6 to 8

2 cups (350 g) manoomin rice

5½ cups (1.3 L) chicken or vegetable stock

½ cup (60 g) diced onion

½ cup (50 g) diced celery

3 sprigs fresh thyme

1 bay leaf

2 teaspoons salt

2 teaspoons freshly cracked black pepper

In a medium pot, add the rice, stock, onion, celery, thyme, bay leaf, salt, and pepper. Bring to a boil over high heat, then reduce the heat to low. Simmer for 40 to 45 minutes, or until the rice is very soft. Adjust the seasoning if necessary, remove the thyme sprigs and bay leaf, and serve immediately. Wild rice should be consumed within four to six days or frozen for up to six months.

Anishinaabeg—Ojibwe, Ojibwa, Chippewa, or Saulteaux

The Anishinaabe People live in the Great Plains, spanning what's now the midwestern U.S. and Canada. The Anishinaabeg are composed of many communities including the Ojibwe, Ojibwa, Chippewa, and Saulteaux. Seven is a sacred number to these people, in part because of the legend of the First Elder. When the First Elder was a small boy, the Seven Grandfathers shared with him the gifts of knowledge. The First Elder then shared his knowledge with the people: wisdom, love, respect, humility, truth, bravery, and the courage to do what is good even when it's difficult. These seven teachings are sacred to the communities who call this world Turtle Island.

According to some communities' legends, the god Gitche Manitou dreamed so intensely, envisioning everything in the world, that it was actually created. I enjoy this story, knowing that when I'm listening to music and daydreaming on my commute to work, I'm not being idle—I'm just thinking up worlds.

In the creation story, when everything flooded and all was nearly lost, the world seemed doomed. But brave, loyal, and very-tired-from-swimming Muskrat clung to a tiny clay piece of the world in its paw. Seeing how tired Muskrat was, Turtle offered to bear the weight of the new world on its back. Their friends helped lift the piece of the world that Muskrat had saved, and there, Turtle Island grew. I love thinking of the world this way, swimming through time and the cosmos, protected by the kindhearted Turtle and friends.

As part of their culinary traditions, the Anishinaabeg grow the three sisters, corn, beans, and squash; they forage foods and hunt for the plentiful freshwater fish in the region, as well as grouse, deer, rabbits, moose, elk, and caribou. Whenever harvesting wild crops, there is an emphasis on taking only what is needed so that the environment doesn't suffer.

Another symbol that's very important to the Anishinaabe People is the medicine wheel: a circle divided into four sections. North is bright white for nighttime, winter, wisdom, elders, sweet grass, and deer; East is yellow for morning, springtime, babies, tobacco, spirit, and eagles; South is red for afternoon, summer, cedar, youth, emotions, and coyote; West is black for evening, autumn, sage, adulthood, physical tasks, and bear. In many medicine wheels, there is a green circle at the center to encourage the balance of these four constitutions. This sacred hoop is a good reminder to focus on the guiding principles of life and balance. In cooking, it reminds me of a round plate that holds a meal with balanced flavors, textures, and colors.

WHENEVER HARVESTING WILD CROPS, THERE IS
AN EMPHASIS ON TAKING ONLY WHAT IS NEEDED SO THAT
THE ENVIRONMENT DOESN'T SUFFER.

STEWED BEANS WITH THYME, SAGE, AND TOMATO

This recipe is an acknowledgment and celebration of Indigenous cultures, histories, and ingredients. Tomatoes, native to South America and used widely by Mayans and Aztecs, were cultivated in what's now Mexico as early as 500 BCE. They pair beautifully with the black, white, and pinto beans in this recipe, which—like all beans—trace back to what's now Peru, more than two thousand years before that. Sage and thyme date back to the ancient Egyptians.

These foods and herbs eventually made their ways into the recipes of many Native American communities across what's now the U.S., and they still stand the test of time. To taste this dish the way Indigenous people would have, get your tomatoes in season and your herbs from the garden, and use homemade stock. This recipe will remind you that rustic, unfussy meals can bring just as much nourishment and pleasure as anything we'd now term new or gourmet.

Serves 6 to 8

3 tablespoons canola oil

1 medium onion, peeled and diced

2 cloves garlic, peeled and minced

¼ cup (30 g) diced carrot

¼ cup (25 g) diced celery

1 bay leaf

4 sprigs fresh thyme

1 tablespoon chopped fresh sage leaves

3 teaspoons salt

3 teaspoons freshly cracked black pepper

1 (14-ounce/420 ml) can diced tomatoes with juice

1½ cups (255 g) cooked pinto beans

1 cup (180 g) cooked white beans

1 cup (185 g) cooked black beans

2 cups (480 ml) chicken stock, or as needed

In a medium pot over medium heat, add the oil. When the oil is hot, add the onion, garlic, carrot, celery, bay leaf, thyme, and sage. Begin to sweat the vegetables, stirring occasionally, for about 5 minutes. Add 2 teaspoons of the salt and 2 teaspoons of the pepper and continue to sweat the vegetables for another 5 minutes, or until soft. Next, deglaze the pan with the tomatoes and their juice until the liquid has evaporated, scraping up any bits that have stuck to the bottom of the pot. Add the pinto, white, and black beans. Cover the beans with the stock. Add more stock if necessary. Increase the heat to high. Bring to a boil, then lower the heat to low and allow to simmer for 1 hour, or until the beans are tender. Add the remaining 1 teaspoon salt and 1 teaspoon pepper. Once the liquid has thickened, remove from the heat, adjust the seasoning if necessary, remove the thyme sprigs, and serve immediately.

SUMMER CORN AND SQUASH

Every summer when I was a kid, my family would load up the car and drive to my grandmother's home in Cortez, Colorado—known for Mesa Verde National Park. We'd take the back roads through the rural, southwestern part of the state, and it seemed to lead us on a new adventure every time. We'd stop at the once-thriving, now-abandoned Ismay Trading Post, a farmers' market that was in the early 1900s a general store, post office, and tire-repair shop.

Local farmers would sell us melons, squash, and other vine-ripe vegetables, and when we arrived at our grandmother's house, she'd start cooking. Here's her traditional family recipe, which showcases the rich and tender squash and the pure magic of late-summer corn. Again, it's a reminder that some of the most delicious dishes in the world are the simplest—grown with care, prepared with intention, and served with love.

Serves 6 to 8

3 tablespoons canola oil

1 medium yellow onion, peeled and diced

4 cups (560 g) fresh or frozen corn kernels

4 cups (460 g) sliced yellow squash

4 cups (460 g) sliced zucchini

1 teaspoon salt

1 teaspoon freshly cracked black pepper

½ cup (25 g) chopped fresh flat-leaf parsley, for garnish

In a large sauté pan over medium heat, add the oil. When the oil is hot, add the onion and corn and sweat, stirring often, for about 10 minutes. The key here is to bring out their natural sweetness by extracting as much sugar as possible from the corn and onion while they soften. If the vegetables are caramelizing too quickly, add ¼ cup (60 ml) water to slow the process. Add the squash and zucchini along with the salt and pepper. Cover the pan with a lid and continue to cook until the squash is tender and wilted, 25 to 30 minutes, checking often. If the vegetables are caramelizing too quickly, add another ¼ cup (60 ml) water to slow the process. Remove from the heat, adjust the seasoning if necessary, garnish with the parsley, and serve immediately.

SUMMER SQUASH MASH

There are many variations to this Indigenous dish that lands squarely between a comfort food and a light summer side. Think of it as the ideal alternative to mashed potatoes, which uses the same technique as the mashed beans recipe on page 114. Native cuisines rely heavily on creative approaches to using staple ingredients, and this dish is a perfect example. Mashed squash is substantial enough to accompany grilled meats and light enough to serve alongside summery salads and vegetarian lunches; switch up your squash, and you'll have an entirely different flavor. Here I call for a mix of yellow squash and zucchini to honor tradition, but it also works well with Zephyr squash, a hybrid that lends itself to quick cooking. Zephyrs have a firm texture that's still soft enough to mash, with a flavor between yellow crookneck, acorn, and delicata. Choose whatever variety is your favorite; just make sure all the water from the squash evaporates completely as you cook it so you get the smooth, thick texture that makes this dish so tasty and decadent-feeling.

Serves 6 to 8

3 tablespoons canola oil

4 yellow squash, peeled and diced

2 zucchini, diced

1 shallot, peeled and minced

1 clove garlic, peeled and minced

1 tablespoon salt

1 tablespoon freshly cracked black pepper

4 cups (960 ml) water, dry white wine, or chicken or vegetable stock, or as needed

3 tablespoons unsalted butter

In a large, heavy-bottom pan over medium heat, add the oil. When the oil is hot, add the squash, zucchini, shallot, garlic, salt, and pepper. Sweat the vegetables, stirring occasionally, until all the moisture from the vegetables has evaporated. Next, add 1 cup (240 ml) of the liquid (the water, wine, or stock) while the squash continues to cook. Make sure the squash doesn't brown. When the liquid has evaporated, about 10 minutes, add some more liquid, 1 cup (240 ml) at a time, and cook until the squash is fork-tender, about another 5 minutes. Note: You may not use all the liquid. Remove the pan from the heat. Using a potato masher, mash the squash. Stir in the butter. Continue to mash until smooth. Adjust the seasoning if necessary and serve immediately.

SUNCHOKE AND POTATO PUREE

We've talked earlier about mashed beans (page 114) and squash (page 130) as a substitute for mashed potatoes, but if you don't want to stray too far from that classic favorite, here's a wonderful alternative. The addition of sunchokes and substitution of coconut milk bring some classic Indigenous ingredients, though of course only the sunchokes are a Native American tradition. Sunchokes are tubers, like potatoes and turnips, with a nutty, artichoke-adjacent flavor. For centuries, Native Americans in North America have relied on sunchokes as a staple ingredient; they grow wild across nearly every state in what's now the U.S. Also known as Jerusalem artichokes, they've been gaining in popularity in recent years; you'll likely see them at your local farmers' market or produce stand. Substitute them for any recipe that calls for potatoes, or, as I've done here, combine the two for the perfect blend of the familiar and less expected. This'll be a delicious side for virtually any meal, but it's my go-to alongside braised meats and vegetables.

Serves 4 to 6

1½ pounds (650 g) peeled and chopped sunchokes (Jerusalem artichokes)

1 cup (140 g) peeled and diced russet potato

2 teaspoons salt

2 teaspoons freshly cracked black pepper

¼ cup (55 g) cold unsalted butter, diced

⅓ cup (75 ml) coconut milk

In a medium pot, add the sunchokes and potato and enough water to cover. Bring to a boil over high heat, then lower the heat to low and simmer until the sunchokes and potato are fork-tender, about 15 minutes. Remove from the heat and drain. Return the sunchokes and potato to the pot and add the salt and pepper. Over low heat, using a rubber spatula, mash the sunchokes and potato while adding the butter little by little. This will evaporate the moisture. Keep incorporating the butter and stirring until there is little steam. Next, transfer the mashed sunchokes and potato to a food processor. While pureeing, slowly drizzle in the coconut milk. Puree until smooth. Adjust the seasoning if necessary and serve.

WILTED DANDELION, MUSTARD, AND SPINACH GREENS

Native American cuisine doesn't generally include raw leafy greens, though greens do appear in traditional recipes: usually cooked and added to soups and fillings. This recipe lands somewhere in the middle, serving the greens fresh but wilted. I love the vibrant pop of color, the sweet, bitter flavor of the greens along with tart, lemony sumac. It's the perfect pick-me-up for earthy greens, and since sumac berries grow wild in what's now the forty-eight contiguous United States, sumac shows up in the recipes of pretty much every Native community with history here. I also love the versatility of this dish—it can be served alongside any hot or cold main dish, with any meat, wild rice, or vegetable recipe. Or—if you really want to flout tradition—under a fried egg for breakfast with my Blue Cornmeal (page 98). I've chosen mustard greens for their peppery spice, dandelion greens for their earthy bitterness, and spinach leaves for their balancing sweetness. Swap out whatever greens you have on hand; this recipe is nothing if not versatile. Be sure to sweat your shallots well to release all their natural sugar.

Serves 4 to 6

3 tablespoons canola oil

1 shallot, peeled and diced

1 clove garlic, peeled and minced

1 teaspoon salt

1 teaspoon freshly cracked black pepper

Vegetable stock, as needed

5 cups (300 g) dandelion greens

2 cups (140 g) mustard greens

2 cups (40 g) spinach leaves

2 teaspoons ground sumac

In a large, heavy-bottom sauté pan over medium heat, add the oil. When the oil is hot, add the shallot, garlic, salt, and pepper. Cook until the shallot is translucent, 5 to 10 minutes, being careful not to burn the garlic. Add a little stock if necessary to deglaze the pan, scraping up any bits stuck to the bottom. Add the dandelion, mustard, and spinach greens and allow them to cook, stirring occasionally, to evenly wilt the greens. Add the sumac and stir, making sure the sumac is distributed throughout the leaves. Cook down until the greens are fully wilted, about 2 minutes. Remove from the heat, adjust the seasoning if necessary, and serve immediately.

Zuni

The Zuni, or Ashiwi, live in New Mexico, where their two-story adobe homes were traditionally constructed from clay. This building technique has been adopted all across the Southwest in stucco buildings and residences, because adobe is an outstanding building material in the desert heat; it stays cool in the summer and remains insulated throughout cold nights. It's a misconception that the desert is always warm—believe me, it gets very cold after the last burst of sunset fades.

The Zuni are a matrilineal society who farm colorful ancestral maize. Because water is a scarce resource in the region, their traditions include a rain blessing ceremony called Shalako, which is held every winter during solstice. Each year, the community leaders choose which family will host the event—a choice that determines who will dress in the regalia of the towering birdlike figure of the Shalako. The ceremony reenacts the origin story of the Zuni, thanking the rain for all it gives, and wishing good health and blessings on all the homes, plants, and animals that surround them.

The Zuni are also talented stonesmiths and craftspeople, known widely for their jewelry. Their designs are admired for their precise geometric patterns using stones, usually without any silver inlay between the turquoise, coral, black onyx, or white opal. Snake designs are also unique to their artwork, a symbol that's believed to keep them connected with higher powers.

As far as their culinary traditions go, Zuni recipes for pozole, chicken with rice, and chili pair well with the puffed bread rolls baked in a beehive-shaped horno mud oven; that tradition is still common, though the rolls can be baked in a typical kitchen oven. What's most specific to their culinary history is their salt: it has a light powdery texture because it is dried from the nearby Zuni Salt Lake. Water and salt, two essential elements of the Zuni's desert home, are sacred in their ceremonies and central to their cuisine.

WATER AND SALT, TWO ESSENTIAL ELEMENTS OF THE ZUNI'S
DESERT HOME, ARE SACRED IN THEIR CEREMONIES AND CENTRAL
TO THEIR CUISINE.

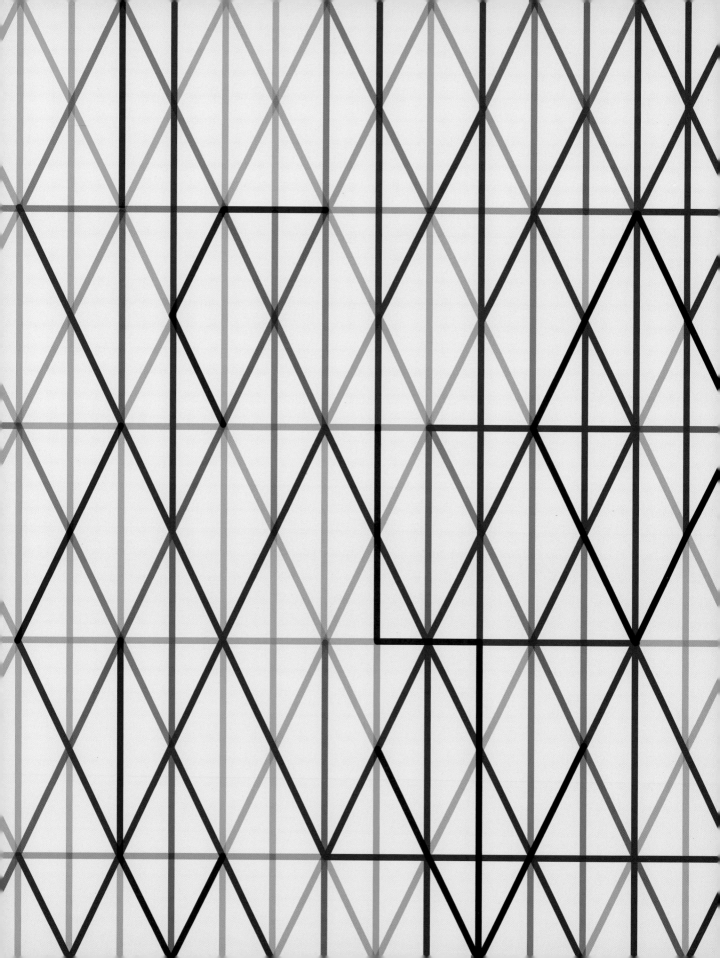

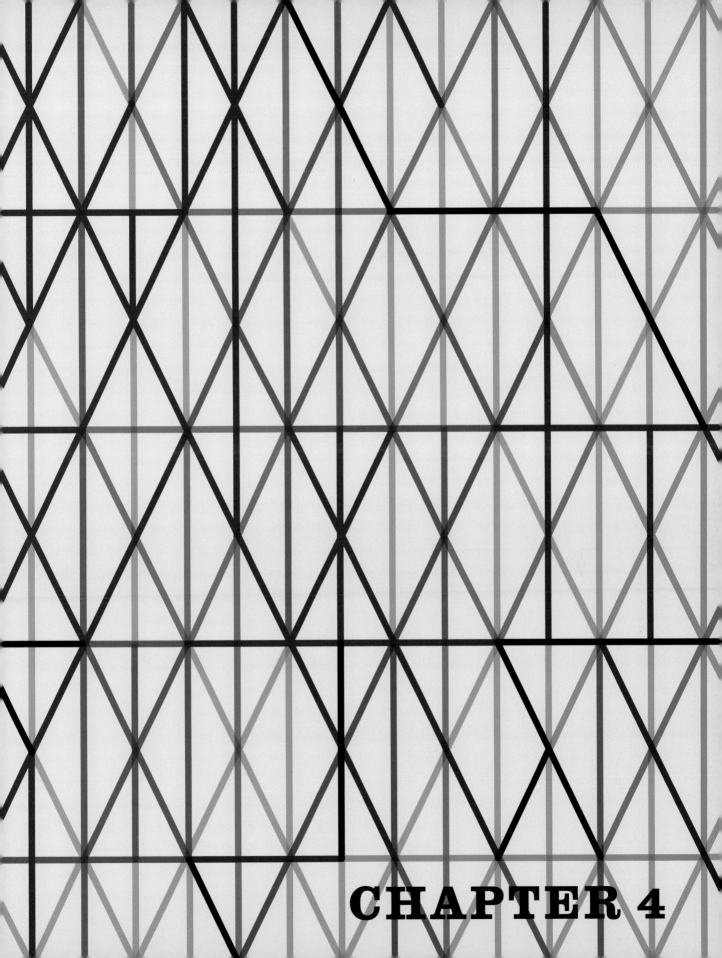

CHAPTER 4

Land and Sea

BEEF

Grilled Beef Tenderloin with Juniper Sauce 142

Southern Ute Breaded Beef with Butter
  and Sage Sauce 144

Stewed Beef with Golden Beets 148

Sumac-Braised Beef Short Ribs 152

BISON

Bison Burgers with Caramelized Sweet
  Onions 154

Braised Bison Short Ribs 158

Chocolate Bison Chili 160

CHICKEN

Braised Chicken with Sage and
  Chokecherry Sauce 164

Cedar Berry–Rubbed Roasted Chicken 166

Golden Chicken Tamales 170

Green Chili Chicken Pozole 174

Saguaro Seed–Crusted Chicken Thighs 176

Stewed Chicken with Golden Tomatoes 180

Grilled Rabbit with Prickly Pear Barbecue
   Sauce 218

Seared Rabbit Loin with Sunchokes 222

FISH AND SHELLFISH

Alaskan King Salmon with Crushed Pecans 226

Cedar Plank Sockeye Salmon 228

Cornmeal-Crusted Walleye with Roasted Corn and
   Green Chilies 234

Makah Crab Boil 238

Pacific Halibut Cakes with Caper Mayonnaise 242

Pan-Roasted Cumin-Crusted Sablefish 244

Sautéed Garlic Spot Prawns 246

People sometimes ask me why I don't include bison in more of my recipes. There are two reasons: the first is that I believe food should be accessible to everyone. Bison is expensive, and therefore culturally divisive; beef is more available, so I use it more often. It's the same reason my recipes call for chicken rather than the wild turkey traditionally hunted by the Mohawk, Onondaga, and Shawnee; the ptarmigan hunted by Eyak, Inuit, and Ontario First Nations; or the grouse hunted by the Cree, Mistassini, Kutchin, and Waswanipi peoples. Many of the foods that were once locally abundant simply aren't any longer—and these recipes are meant to be approachable for home chefs in any city or town.

Second, it's a mistake to believe that the 574 currently federally recognized Native nations and 63 state-recognized communities originating from what's now the continental U.S. and Alaska are Plains communities with a history of hunting bison. The wide and varied recipes that follow are a tribute to Native American recipes from the East, West, and Gulf Coasts, the Midwest, Northwest, and Southwest. I've also included a few to show you some of the Indigenous histories behind now-familiar recipes. Ever had chicken and dumplings? Try my Lamb Soup with Blue Corn Dumplings (page 194). Like fresh-cracked crab? Try my Makah Crab Boil (page 238). This is a chance to taste where your favorites first came from.

Of course, thousands of years ago, many of the meats in these dishes wouldn't have existed on this continent. But as cultures evolved or were forced to change, recipes also evolved to incorporate new sources of protein like chicken, pork, beef, and lamb—which I'm especially honored to share. Lamb dishes are connected to my own personal history, including the Braised Lamb Shanks with Navajo Steam Corn (page 192), which reminds me of meals with my grandmother and the Navajo legend that tells of a dense fog that lasted for days. People couldn't see in the mist and were unable to hunt or gather food. They began to worry. But when the fog finally lifted, herds of sheep were grazing on the land: a gift of sustenance for the future.

You'll see that I've adjusted some ancient tastes and techniques to appeal to modern palates and kitchens. What was once stewed is now braised, often with wine. What was once cooked over open flames is now grilled. Foods roasted underground have oven-friendly options, and the salmon originally held over a fire with cedar spears is now cooked on fragrant planks. My recipes also rarely ask you to cook an entire animal, as Indigenous communities would have. Now it's just as easy to get a loin or a shank, thighs or ribs. Though if you're interested in the experience of cooking an entire bird, try my Grilled Duck with Apple and Sage (page 186). Cooking "nose to tail" is a meaningful way to honor the life of an animal.

For me, what's most important about these meat and seafood dishes is that they reflect the often-forgotten history of foods so many people know and love: tamales, smoked salmon, corn dumplings, chili, breaded fish, and so many more dishes that have their roots in Native American cuisine. This chapter invites you to adjust your definition of Native American food and to try things you might be nervous to attempt without a trusted guide. These land and sea recipes are simple, because fussiness didn't exist in ancient Indigenous culinary traditions. And like all my dishes, these are meant to pair with fresh herbs and produce. Find what's in season, celebrate what grows locally, and work from there. It also can't hurt to make friends with your local butcher and fishmonger.

GRILLED BEEF TENDERLOIN
WITH JUNIPER SAUCE

Juniper grows wild in the high deserts of the western side of the continent. It's been included for thousands of years in the recipes of many Native American communities. Honoring that tradition, this recipe takes a well-known American dish—grilled steak, or filet mignon—and pairs it with the tart,

piney, slightly citrus flavor of juniper. I generally reach for dried juniper, but if you're using fresh berries, you'll need to adjust for their more intense flavor. A more traditional pairing would feature bison, which you can substitute here, or any other cut or preparation of beef.

Serves 6

½ cup (65 g) chopped shallot

1 clove garlic, peeled

¼ cup (13 g) fresh flat-leaf parsley, plus 1 tablespoon chopped parsley, for garnish

1 tablespoon salt

1 tablespoon freshly cracked black pepper

1½ cups (360 ml) canola oil

6 (8-ounce/225 g) beef tenderloins

Juniper Sauce, recipe follows

JUNIPER SAUCE
Makes approximately 4 cups (960 ml)

2 tablespoons canola oil

1 teaspoon chopped fresh rosemary

1 small onion, peeled and diced

1 clove garlic, peeled and chopped

1 teaspoon fresh thyme leaves

2 teaspoons ground juniper berries

1 cup (240 ml) dry red wine, optional

4 cups (960 ml) beef stock

Salt and freshly cracked black pepper

2 tablespoons arrowroot powder

Prepare and preheat an outdoor grill to high heat.

In a blender, add the shallot, 1 clove garlic, ¼ cup (13 g) parsley, salt, and pepper and puree. With the blender running, slowly drizzle in 1½ cups (360 ml) oil, until smooth. In a medium bowl, add the puree, then add the beef tenderloins, coating each one. Allow to marinate for at least 1 hour. Arrange the seasoned tenderloins on the grill. Grill on each side for 3 to 4 minutes for medium-rare. Remove from the heat and tent the grilled tenderloins with aluminum foil. Allow to rest for 5 to 6 minutes before serving with a side of juniper sauce and a sprinkling of chopped parsley.

In a medium saucepot over low heat, add 2 tablespoons oil. When the oil is hot, add the rosemary, onion, 1 clove chopped garlic, thyme, and juniper berries and stir well to combine. Sauté, stirring often, until the onions are soft; do not burn the garlic. Increase the heat to medium. Add the wine (if using) and reduce until dry. Add the stock, season with salt and pepper, and bring to a boil. Remove from the heat and transfer the contents to a blender (caution: liquid will be hot). Puree for 5 to 7 minutes, or until smooth. Reserve ¼ cup (60 ml) of the puree and pour the rest back into the pot. In a small bowl, combine the reserved puree with the arrowroot. Stir well to make a slurry and add to the pot. Stir well to combine and thicken the sauce. Adjust the seasoning if necessary and serve.

SOUTHERN UTE BREADED BEEF
WITH BUTTER AND SAGE SAUCE

The Southern Ute were a large community who traditionally lived and hunted across several states in what's now the American West and Southwest. They often ate elk, deer, and bison, which would've been the traditional meat in this dish—also cooked over a fire and seasoned with fresh herbs. My version substitutes beef, which stays juicier than bison when sliced thin, seared on high heat, and finished in the oven. Because bison is so lean, this recipe is one of the few exceptions to the rule that beef and bison can be used interchangeably in my recipes. Stick with beef for this one. Fire, fresh herbs, and meat are the Indigenous traditions here—but bread crumbs, warm butter, and wine bring it into this century and, I suspect, into your list of home-cooked favorites.

Serves 6 to 8

¼ cup (60 ml) canola oil

2 cups (250 g) all-purpose flour

3 eggs, beaten

2 cups (200 g) bread crumbs

1 cup (50 g) chopped fresh flat-leaf parsley

2 to 2½ pounds (910 g to 1.2 kg) top round steaks, thinly sliced to ⅛ to ¼ inch (3 to 6 mm) to make 8 beef cutlets

Salt and freshly cracked black pepper

Butter and Sage Sauce, recipe follows

Preheat the oven to 350°F (175°C).

In a large sauté pan over medium heat, add ¼ cup (60 ml) oil. While the oil is heating, spread the flour on a large plate. Pour the eggs into a wide bowl. Combine the bread crumbs with the parsley and spread on another plate. Season the cutlets with salt and pepper and dredge in the flour, shaking off excess. Next, dip the cutlets into the eggs and then dredge in the bread crumbs to evenly coat. When the oil is hot, place the breaded cutlets into the sauté pan and sear both sides until golden brown. Note: You may need to sauté in batches. Remove the cutlets and transfer to a baking sheet. Place in the oven and bake for 8 to 10 minutes, or until cooked through. Remove from the oven and serve with the butter and sage sauce.

BUTTER AND SAGE SAUCE
Makes approximately ¾ cup (180 ml)

1 teaspoon canola oil

½ cup (70 g) diced shallot

1 teaspoon dried sage leaves

½ cup (120 ml) dry white wine

1 cup (2 sticks/225 g) cold unsalted butter, diced

Juice of 1 lemon

2 tablespoons fresh sage leaves, cut into thin, long strips (chiffonade)

1 teaspoon salt

1 teaspoon freshly cracked black pepper

In a medium sauté pan over medium heat, add 1 tablespoon oil. When the oil is hot, add the shallot and dried sage and sweat the shallot until softened, about 5 minutes. Deglaze the pan with the wine or ½ cup (120 ml) water, scraping up any bits stuck to the bottom of the pan, and cook until the liquid has evaporated. Reduce the heat to low. While whisking, add the butter a little at a time. Once all the butter has been added, quickly add the lemon juice, followed by the fresh sage. Season the sauce with 1 teaspoon salt and 1 teaspoon pepper and serve.

Ute

Winters can be harsh for this community of many bands that spans across the region now covered by Colorado, Utah, Wyoming, Nevada, New Mexico, and Arizona. Every year, when the first thunder of spring crashes, members of the Ute community emerge from their winter homes for the Bear Dance. After a long season stuck indoors, sheltering from the cold and practicing songs, it's a joyous occasion. People let loose and celebrate the beginning of spring during this special event that showcases horse racing, gambling, feasts, and dancing. Traditionally, a large meat and vegetable stew is prepared over the open fire for the whole community to share.

The Ute are a group who historically span the basins and mountains of the Rockies, so their varied foodways reflect the diverse elevations and terrains of the region. In ancient times, they hunted elk and trapped smaller game that lived in the wilds of their large territory. They also made tools and clothing from the hides, always honoring the entire animal. Many of these traditions continue today, as does the guiding principle to never overharvest when gathering plants for food. For this reason, they rotate which areas they harvest and which areas they hunt. In addition to growing crops, the Ute often cook with foods foraged from wild plants including amaranth, alliums, dandelion, and wild rice.

In 2012, the Ancestral Puebloan site of Chimney Rock in southwestern Colorado was designated a protected United States national monument. It was a great moment in history, honoring the spiritual center for a robust network of Ute communities that were built in the shadow of its natural spire, revered because of a phenomenon called the lunar standstill. Every eighteen years, the moon reaches the farthest point from the earth in its orbit; when it does, it rises and sets to the far north and the moon is framed in the center of the ancient tall stones.

IN ADDITION TO GROWING CROPS, THE UTE OFTEN COOK
WITH FOODS FORAGED FROM WILD PLANTS INCLUDING AMARANTH,
ALLIUMS, DANDELION, AND WILD RICE.

So many modern recipes are about fast, convenient meals, but there's something to be said for the experience of preparing and eating slow-cooked dishes. Your home filling up with the scent of fresh herbs and spices, stewed meat growing tender and savory as the afternoon rolls into evening. I love the simple luxury of a leisurely meal on an unhurried day—and this recipe is a fine choice for it. I was first introduced to this cozy, hearty recipe by the local communities at a culinary conference in Anchorage, Alaska, and I made it for my friends and family as soon as I arrived back home. This is another nourishing dish in which you can substitute bison or other lean game such as elk or wild boar for beef. Slow cooking means whatever protein you choose, the meat will end up extremely tender while the taste is intensified from the hearty vegetables and herbs. I find that the robust flavors of bay leaves, thyme, and tomato pair exceptionally well with big-game meats, which are often stronger and saltier than beef. Regardless of what cubed meat you desire, this dish will turn out splendidly each and every time. For this particular recipe, I like using golden beets, given their inviting color and milder flavor. When roasted, they take on a wonderful sweetness to balance the earthiness. Like all root vegetables, beets are common in Native American recipes—though the golden ones appear most often in recipes of Pacific Northwest communities. Swap beets for potatoes in any slow-cooked recipe for a more complex flavor, enhanced nutritional value, and a bright splash of color.

Serves 6 to 8

3 tablespoons canola oil

3 pounds (1.4 kg) beef chuck, cubed

Salt and freshly cracked black pepper

1 medium onion, peeled and diced

2 green bell peppers, seeded and diced

2 stalks celery, diced

2 bay leaves

4 sprigs fresh thyme

2 teaspoons ground coriander

3 tablespoons tomato paste

1 cup (240 ml) dry red wine or beef stock

8 medium golden beets, peeled

1 cup (165 g) crushed tomatoes

3 cups (720 ml) beef stock

Preheat the oven to 350°F (175°C).

In a Dutch oven over high heat, add the oil. While the oil is heating, season the beef with salt and pepper. Working in batches, add some of the beef to the hot oil and sear all sides. Once browned, remove, set aside, and add the next batch of beef.

After all the beef has browned, set the beef aside, reduce the heat to low, and add the onion, bell peppers, celery, bay leaves, thyme, and coriander.

Sweat the vegetables until the onions are soft and begin to caramelize, about 10 minutes. Using a spoon, clear a space in the middle of the vegetables and add the tomato paste directly to the hot surface of the pot. Allow the paste to brown and form a crust (takes about 2 minutes; be careful not to burn the paste). Then add the wine or 1 cup (240 ml) stock to deglaze the pot and stir so the paste is incorporated into the vegetables. Allow the liquid to evaporate completely.

RECIPE CONTINUES

Return the seared beef to the pot along with the beets, crushed tomatoes, and 3 cups (720 ml) stock. Increase the heat to high and bring to a boil. Once boiling, remove from the heat, cover, and place in the oven. Cook for 2½ hours.

After 2½ hours, remove the beef and beets from the sauce and set aside. Place the Dutch oven back on the stove over medium heat. Allow the sauce to reduce by about one-quarter. Return the beef and beets to the pot and reduce the sauce by another one-quarter. Remove from the heat and discard the bay leaves and thyme sprigs. Adjust the seasoning if necessary and arrange the beef and beets on a serving platter along with the sauce. Serve immediately.

The delicately fragrant bay leaf is a common ingredient in Native American cooking, especially for communities in the Pacific Northwest.

SUMAC-BRAISED BEEF
SHORT RIBS

Braising sounds fancy, but it's simple: sear your meat, then cook it slowly in moist heat as opposed to dry heat like a roast. It's a centuries-old technique that can make tougher meats (including bison) fork-tender. This is not a completely traditional recipe, especially given the deglazing with red wine. But this simple one-pot meal is fall-off-the-bone tender and outright delectable. The sumac, fresh herbs, and root vegetables keep it grounded in tradition, and though this recipe calls for beef short ribs, it's just as delicious with bison short ribs. Think of it as the solution to a no-stress dinner party: all the cooking is done hours ahead of your guests' arrival.

Serves 6 to 8

3 tablespoons canola oil

3 pounds (1.4 kg) boneless beef short ribs, cut into 6-ounce (170 g) strips (the butcher can do this)

Salt and freshly cracked black pepper

2 stems fresh rosemary

2 fresh sage leaves

5 sprigs fresh thyme

2 bay leaves

½ cup (50 g) plus 3 tablespoons ground sumac

1 large onion, peeled and diced

2 medium turnips, cleaned and chopped

2 veal shanks, optional

¼ cup (60 ml) tomato paste

1½ cups (360 ml) dry red wine

1 cup (240 ml) tomato puree

3 cups (720 ml) beef stock

½ cup (18 g) chopped fresh sage leaves, for garnish

Preheat the oven to 350°F (175°C).

In a Dutch oven over high heat, add the oil. While the oil is heating, season the short ribs with salt and pepper. Searing in batches, add about four ribs at a time to the hot oil. Sear all sides of the ribs. Once browned, remove, set aside, and add the next batch of ribs. After all the ribs are browned, set the meat aside, reduce the heat to low, and add the rosemary, 2 sage leaves, thyme, bay leaves, ½ cup (50 g) ground sumac, onion, turnips, veal (if using), and 1 tablespoon each of salt and pepper. Sweat the vegetables until the onions are soft and begin to caramelize, about 10 minutes. Clear a space in the middle of the vegetables and add the tomato paste directly to the hot surface of the pot. Allow the paste to brown and form a crust (takes about 2 minutes; be careful not to burn the paste). Then add the wine or 1½ cups (360 ml) water to deglaze the pot and stir so the paste is incorporated into the vegetables. Allow the wine to evaporate completely. Return the seared ribs to the pot along with the tomato puree and stock. Increase the heat to high and bring to a boil. Once boiling, remove from the heat, cover, and place in the oven. Braise for 2 hours.

After 2 hours, remove the ribs from the sauce and set aside. Place the Dutch oven back on the stove over medium heat. Allow the sauce to reduce by about one-quarter. Return the ribs to the pot and reduce the sauce by another one-quarter. Remove from the heat and discard the rosemary, sage, thyme sprigs, bay leaves, and veal. Adjust the seasoning if necessary and arrange the ribs on a serving platter along with the sauce. Garnish with the remaining 3 tablespoons sumac and the chopped sage just before serving.

BISON BURGERS WITH CARAMELIZED SWEET ONIONS

This recipe works the opposite of many in this book—instead of modernizing a traditional recipe, I'm traditionalizing a modern recipe. Imagine your favorite burger, then swap out the beef patty for ground bison. Ground bison is one of the least expensive ways to try this Indigenous staple, and I give my preparation additional Native American ingredients, topping the burger with caramelized onions seasoned with fresh herbs and juniper berries. Serve bison burgers over wilted greens, alongside any of my salads, or on a fresh-baked brioche bun for a Native American-meets-modern-American classic.

Serves 4

1 pound (455 g) ground bison

2 teaspoons salt

2 teaspoons freshly cracked black pepper

½ cup (25 g) chopped fresh flat-leaf parsley

¼ cup (25 g) grated queso fresco

Caramelized Sweet Onions, recipe follows

4 hamburger buns

Condiments of choice

Prepare and preheat an outdoor grill to high heat.

In a large bowl, add the bison, 2 teaspoons salt, 2 teaspoons pepper, parsley, and queso fresco. Mix well by hand, but do not overmix. Divide evenly and shape into quarter-pound burgers, about ¼ inch (6 mm) thick. Arrange the burgers on the grill and cook 3 to 4 minutes per side for medium-rare (cook longer if you prefer medium-well). Do not touch or press the burgers during the grilling process. The key is to keep the juices inside. Otherwise, the burgers will be dry. Remove the burgers and let rest for a couple minutes. Top with the caramelized sweet onions and serve on buns with any condiments you like.

CARAMELIZED SWEET ONIONS
Makes approximately ½ cup (115 g)

2 teaspoons canola oil

1 large sweet onion, peeled and diced

1 sprig fresh thyme

1 bay leaf

2 teaspoons salt

2 teaspoons freshly cracked black pepper

½ teaspoon ground juniper berries

2 tablespoons agave nectar

In a medium sauté pan over low heat, add the oil. When the oil is hot, add the onion, thyme, bay leaf, 2 teaspoons salt, and 2 teaspoons pepper. Allow the onion to sweat for about 10 minutes, at which time it will begin to caramelize. Deglaze the pan with ¼ cup (60 ml) water and keep sautéing for 15 minutes. If the onions caramelize too quickly, deglaze with another ¼ cup (60 ml) water to slow the cooking process. You want the onions soft and caramelized, not burnt. Add the juniper berries and agave nectar. Stir well to combine, remove from the heat, discard the thyme sprig and bay leaf, and set aside and keep warm.

The American Bison

The American bison is often incorrectly referred to as a buffalo; bison are not true buffalo. According to Prehistoric Fauna (prehistoric-fauna.com), the earliest bison (about 10,000 BCE) roamed the great bison belt—a huge segment of prime grassland from Alaska to northern Mexico. By the early eighteenth century, bison populations exceeded sixty million animals. Unfortunately, they were nearly decimated to extinction by commercial hunting after European contact, and by the late 1800s, only 541 animals were said to remain. Today, there are about thirty thousand bison, mostly in the Rocky Mountain National Park system and in smaller private bison herds raised for conservation and restoration efforts. Some of these herds are raised strictly for the sale of bison meat throughout North America.

North American bison are the heaviest land animals native to North America, and the second tallest; only moose are taller. According to NatureWorks (nhpbs. org/natureworks/americanbison.htm), male bison can weigh between 1,000 and 2,000 pounds (455 and 905 kg) and stand 5 to 6½ feet (1.5 to 2 m) tall. They appear slow-moving but can reach speeds of 35 to 40 mph (55 to 65 kph). Bison can also jump as high as 6 feet (1.8 m) from a standing position.

Bison, like elk and mule deer, are an iconic species with a historic and colorful background in the American West. It can be hard to imagine hunting bison when sixty million of them roamed North America. Today, through conservation efforts mostly funded by hunters, Yellowstone has the largest huntable, free-ranging bison herd in North America. There are also wild herds in Alaska, Arizona, Montana, South Dakota, Utah, Wyoming, the Crow Reservation in Montana, and Canada.

BRAISED BISON SHORT RIBS

Braised short ribs are one of my favorite comfort foods, so I couldn't help but include two recipes for them. This heartier, thicker, wintrier version feels a bit more rustic than the Sumac-Braised Beef Short Ribs (page 152). These also cook a bit longer to allow for the leaner bison, which sometimes needs more time to tenderize. The easiest place to find bone-in bison ribs is from your local butcher.

You may have to pre-order, but the wait will be well worth it. In early Indigenous recipes, centuries before stovetop searing and oven slow-cooking were possible, this would've been a stewed meat recipe. But braising is now as common a technique in Native American households as anywhere else; and after the first time you make these ribs, you'll know why.

Serves 6 to 8

¼ cup (60 ml) canola oil

8 bone-in bison short ribs, about 7½ pounds (3.4 kg)

2 cups (250 g) all-purpose flour

1 medium onion, peeled and diced

2 carrots, diced

2 stalks celery, diced

5 sprigs fresh thyme

2 bay leaves

2 cloves garlic, peeled and minced

2 teaspoons salt

2 teaspoons freshly cracked black pepper

3 tablespoons tomato paste

2 cups (480 ml) dry red wine, optional

2 cups (480 ml) beef stock, or as needed

Preheat the oven to 350°F (175°C).

In a Dutch oven over high heat, add the oil. While the oil is heating, dredge the short ribs in the flour, shaking off excess. Add the ribs to the hot oil. Sear all sides of the short ribs. Once browned, remove and set aside. Reduce the heat to low and add the onion, carrots, celery, thyme, bay leaves, garlic, salt, and pepper. Sweat the vegetables until the onions are soft and begin to caramelize, about 10 minutes.

Clear a space in the middle of the vegetables and add the tomato paste directly to the hot surface of the pot. Allow the paste to brown and form a crust (takes about 2 minutes; be careful not to burn the paste). Then add the wine (if using) to deglaze the pot and stir so the paste is incorporated into the vegetables. Allow the wine to evaporate completely. If you're not using the wine, deglaze the pot with some of the stock, scraping up any bits stuck to the bottom of the pot. Add the stock to the pot, ensuring the vegetables are just covered. Add more stock if necessary. Return the seared ribs to the pot. Increase the heat to high and bring to a boil. Once boiling, remove from the heat, cover, and place in the oven. Braise for 2½ hours.

After 2½ hours, remove the ribs from the sauce and set aside. Remove the thyme sprigs and bay leaves and transfer the contents of the pot to a blender (caution: the liquid will be hot). Puree for 5 minutes, or until smooth. Return the blended contents to the pot and add the ribs. Return to medium heat and let the sauce and ribs reheat. Adjust the seasoning if necessary and serve immediately once the ribs and sauce are hot.

Chocolate has a long, sacred history in Indigenous recipes beginning with the Mayans, Aztecs, and other communities of the Yucatán Peninsula, where cacao beans have always grown wild. Cacao has been integral to Indigenous ceremony and cuisine—from drinks to mole sauces and spice rubs. In 2000, the Chickasaw Nation became the only Native American community to create its own brand of artisanal chocolate; I had the pleasure of visiting Bedré Fine Chocolate several years ago and witnessed firsthand how the company instills their cultural passion into every delicious morsel. This recipe draws on ancient tradition to create a spicy, savory, herbaceous chili with a hint of that bittersweet goodness. This is the kind of fabulous-tasting chili that your friends will remember—and ask you to make again and again.

Serves 6 to 8

1 tablespoon canola oil

1 large onion, peeled and chopped

3 cloves garlic, peeled and minced

1 green bell pepper, seeded and diced

3 sprigs fresh thyme

1 bay leaf

1 pound (455 g) ground bison

Salt and freshly cracked black pepper

1 tablespoon tomato paste

1 teaspoon ground cumin

1 teaspoon ground coriander

2 teaspoons paprika

½ teaspoon cayenne pepper

1 (14-ounce/420 ml) can diced tomatoes with juice

1 (14-ounce/400 g) can kidney beans

3 cups (720 ml) bison or beef stock

1¼ cups (225 g) semisweet chocolate chips

In a heavy stockpot or Dutch oven over medium heat, add the oil. When the oil is hot, add the onion, garlic, bell pepper, thyme, and bay leaf. Sauté until the vegetables are soft, stirring occasionally, about 5 minutes. Add the bison, season with salt and pepper, and sear the meat while breaking it up with a wooden spoon or spatula. Cook for about 8 minutes. Add the tomato paste and allow the paste to brown but not burn. Add the cumin, coriander, paprika, cayenne, and diced tomatoes. Use the juice of the diced tomatoes to deglaze the bottom of the pot. Add the beans and stock and bring to a boil. Note: Do not boil hard or for too long or the beans will tear apart. Allow to boil for about 5 minutes, then reduce the heat to low and simmer. Add the chocolate and allow the chili to reduce until it reaches a nice stew consistency. Adjust the seasoning if necessary, then stir to make sure the melted chocolate is evenly distributed. Remove the thyme sprigs and bay leaf, and serve immediately. This chili can be refrigerated for three to four days or frozen for four to six months.

Chickasaw and Choctaw Nations

Indigenous nations of the eastern woodlands and Southeast, including the fertile Mississippi Valley, make up an incredibly diverse region of agrarian societies and skilled traders including the Cherokee, Muscogee (Miccosukee), Seminole, Chickasaw, Choctaw, and others. Because the Southeast is such a fertile place, most of the communities from this region farmed and cultivated the land centuries ago in astoundingly sophisticated ways.

For example, the Chickasaw's robust civic infrastructure depended on a complex network of trade routes and included food storage buildings, city council houses, and fortresses. For centuries, the Chickasaw People have had a democratic political system where respected elders discuss decisions and review disputes in the community.

While each tribal community has its own heritage and customs, this region is well known for a beloved sport called stickball, which is similar to lacrosse. Stickball is important the way football, baseball, or soccer is for some families. It's a social game sometimes played just for fun; other times there are ceremonial matches; other times, games settle disagreements. A more serious, updated version is all-gender, with an official set of rules, sports regulations, and field dimensions. Similar to Super Bowl parties, stickball championships are more like festivals, flanked by food trucks serving partygoers Indigenous fare while they cheer on their teams.

The Choctaw of this region have a fascinating culinary tradition; their protein staples include turkey—which is native to the Southeast—waterfowl, white-tailed deer, and sometimes bear. Before a hunt, the Choctaw would recite a prayer, asking for the wind to help them get close enough without being detected—because the closer you are when hunting, the less likely you are to cause pain to the animal. After the meat was eaten or preserved, bones would be used to make tools, and hides to make all kinds of things—including balls for games. Similar to the Cherokee, the Choctaw incorporated sports like stickball into their celebratory events.

The Choctaw are a matriarchal society, emphasizing a spiritual reverence for acts of nurture and caretaking. In their ancestral homelands, they cared for oak and hickory orchards; the nuts of these trees were harvested and pressed to create savory vegan butters to garnish cornbread and other dishes. Today the Chickasaw and Choctaw Peoples carry on ancestral traditions of joy and celebration, eating Indigenous foods like corn and roasted meat, and getting together to enjoy a friendly game and a satisfying meal.

BECAUSE THE SOUTHEAST IS SUCH A FERTILE PLACE, MOST OF
THE COMMUNITIES FROM THIS REGION FARMED AND CULTIVATED THE
LAND CENTURIES AGO IN ASTOUNDINGLY SOPHISTICATED WAYS.

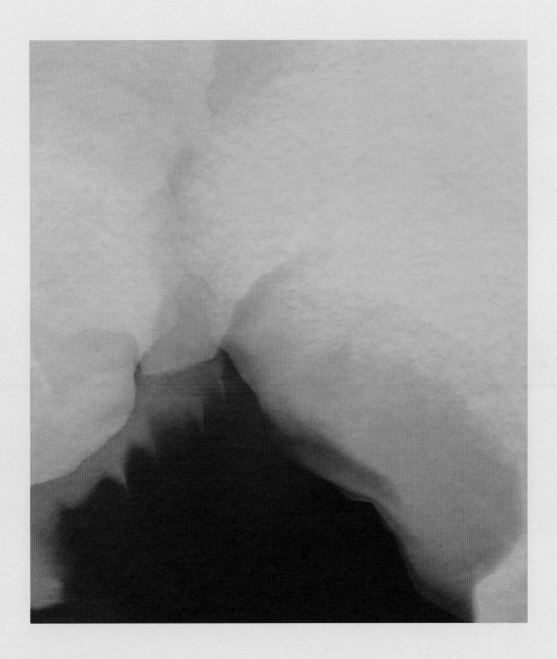

BRAISED CHICKEN WITH
SAGE AND CHOKECHERRY SAUCE

I love braised chicken thighs and legs because they're flavorful, easy to prepare, and the perfect vehicle for the chokecherry sauce I've created as the star of this dish. Chokecherries were a staple food for Indigenous communities who lived on the plains and prairies of North America, but they're bitter if eaten raw. Chokecherries are particularly common in recipes passed down from the Nez Perce, who cooked or dried them to offset the bitterness, and also hunted bison where chokecherries grow wild; their recipes would pair them, but mine calls for chicken thighs and legs instead, which are less expensive and easier to find than bison and are delicious with the chokecherry preserves. Think of this dish as a new take on the familiar turkey-cranberry combination. A comforting, cozy, autumnal recipe that'll make you want to set your table in front of a roaring fire.

Serves 4

3 tablespoons canola oil

4 skin-on bone-in chicken thighs

4 skin-on bone-in chicken legs

1 small onion, peeled and diced

2 cloves garlic, peeled and minced

4 sprigs fresh thyme

1 bay leaf

1 tablespoon chopped fresh sage leaves

1 teaspoon salt

1 teaspoon freshly cracked black pepper

1 cup (240 ml) cranberry juice

¼ cup (60 ml) chokecherry preserves

2 cups (480 ml) chicken stock

Whole sage leaves, for garnish, optional

In a large, heavy-bottom sauté pan over high heat, add the oil. When the oil is hot, add the chicken and sear on all sides until crusted. Remove the chicken and lower the heat to medium-low. Add the onion, garlic, thyme, bay leaf, chopped sage, salt, and pepper and sauté until the onion is translucent, about 5 minutes. Add the cranberry juice and deglaze the pan, scraping up any bits stuck to the bottom. As soon as the cranberry juice is cooked off, return the chicken to the pan. Add the chokecherry preserves and stock. Stir to incorporate, reduce the heat to medium-low, and cover the pan. Allow the chicken to braise for 30 to 35 minutes, or until the internal temperature of the chicken reaches 165°F (75°C). Uncover the pan and let the liquid reduce by half. Adjust the seasoning if necessary, remove the thyme sprigs and bay leaf, and serve the chicken immediately with the sauce spooned over the top. Garnish with whole sage leaves, if desired.

CEDAR BERRY–RUBBED ROASTED CHICKEN

Many Indigenous communities were agricultural communities, including the Pueblos of what are now Arizona and New Mexico. When chickens were first imported and introduced to Native American recipes in the late sixteenth century, thousand-year-old recipes began to change and pass down differently to younger generations. This basic recipe for roasting a whole chicken was passed down to me by my grandmother, and I'm passing it to you. I've added a cedar berry marinade to honor the Indigenous tradition of incorporating nutrient-packed seeds and berries. The mild, woodsy, slightly piney flavor pairs deliciously with sage and rosemary, elevating a simple roast chicken to something simply delectable.

Serves 6 to 8

2 tablespoons ground dried cedar berries

2 tablespoons dried sage leaves

2 tablespoons chopped fresh rosemary

2 tablespoons salt

2 tablespoons freshly cracked black pepper

3 tablespoons canola oil

1 whole fryer chicken

Butcher's twine, as needed

Preheat the oven to 450°F (230°C).

In a small bowl, add the cedar berries, sage, rosemary, salt, and pepper. Slowly whisk in the oil until incorporated. Rub the marinade liberally over all parts of the chicken. Using some butcher's twine, tie the legs and wings so the chicken stays in shape (see page 168). Transfer the chicken to a roasting pan and place in the oven. Roast for 20 minutes, then reduce the temperature to 350°F (175°C) and continue roasting for another 40 minutes, or until the internal temperature reaches 165°F (75°C), basting every 10 minutes or so with the juices for a moist, flavorful bird. Use a meat thermometer to check right where the leg connects to the body. Let the chicken rest for about 20 minutes before carving, which you can do when serving, or remove all the meat from the bones for later use.

Trussing a Bird

Tying up your bird, such as a chicken or duck,
before roasting is a basic culinary skill that can be accomplished
in four traditional steps using some butcher's twine.

Step One

Begin by placing about 3 feet (90 cm) of twine
under the bird just behind the wings. Pull the twine
over and around the wings.

Step Two

Cross the twine underneath the tip of the breast
and pull the wings snug against the bird.

Step Three

Wrap the twine over and then under the legs
and pull the legs tight.

Step Four

Turn the bird over and cross the twine over the
tail of the bird. Pull tight and tie off with a knot.
Remove the extra twine with scissors.

GOLDEN CHICKEN TAMALES

The Aztecs were cooking tamales underground, in ash pits, as far back as 700 BCE—centuries before Spanish explorers set sail for this continent. My recipe, "golden" for the gold masa instead of blue cornmeal, modernizes the ancient Aztec tradition with the always-delicious combination of tender chicken, sweet corn, fragrant smoke, and spicy green chilies. Culinary ash adds a smoky depth of flavor from the burned branches of juniper or chamisa; it also keeps the cornmeal from crumbling. Substitute baking powder if you prefer. It's always been tradition in Native American recipes to fill tamales with meat—but as I noted earlier, chicken didn't make its way into Indigenous recipes until the 1500s. Pork began to influence Indigenous cooking around the same time, and it's a delicious substitution. This dish, for all those reasons, is one of the best examples of old and new. Tamales are also the perfect gossip food, inviting you to open this book alongside your family and friends and make tamales together while sharing stories and news.

Makes 16 tamales

Golden Masa, recipe follows

½ pound (225 g) dried corn husks, soaked in water for at least 4 hours, then patted dry

Chicken Filling, recipe follows

Red chili sauce, for serving, optional

Spread a thin layer (about ¼ inch/6 mm thick) of golden masa evenly along the center of the largest and widest part of each husk. Spread about 2 tablespoons of the chicken filling in the middle of each husk, on top of the golden masa. Take each side of the husk and fold up and over toward the center. Do the same with the ends, as if creating a little package. Turn over each tamale so the ends don't open. Add a little water to a large pot or pan and place over low heat. Arrange the tamales in a steamer basket (stainless steel vegetable steamers work well); you may need to steam in batches. Cover the pot or pan and steam for 90 minutes. Remove the tamales from the steamer and serve immediately with red chili sauce, if desired. Tamales typically freeze well. Place any leftover tamales in freezer bags or airtight freezer containers and freeze them for up to six months.

GOLDEN MASA
Makes approximately 2 cups (600 g)

2 ½ cups (450 g) golden masa harina corn flour

½ teaspoon culinary ash or baking powder

2 teaspoons salt

½ cup (105 g) lard

2 cups (480 ml) chicken stock

Using a stand mixer (or good ol' fashioned elbow grease), combine the corn flour, culinary ash, salt, and lard until well mixed. The objective is to achieve a very smooth and moist dough. Once the mixture is blended, add the stock about ¼ cup (60 ml) at a time while continuing to mix. Don't allow the dough to become too wet. The mixture should resemble a thick, pliable paste. Cover and set aside.

CHICKEN FILLING
Makes approximately 4 cups (900 g)

3 tablespoons canola oil

6 boneless skinless chicken thighs

1 small onion, peeled and diced

2 cloves garlic, peeled and minced

1 bay leaf

2 teaspoons salt

2 teaspoons freshly cracked black pepper

½ cup (75 g) roasted green chilies (see page 32), diced

4 cups (960 ml) chicken stock

In a Dutch oven over high heat, add the oil. When the oil is hot, add the chicken and sear on all sides until browned. Remove the chicken and set aside. Reduce the heat to low and add the onion, garlic, bay leaf, salt, and pepper. Sweat the onions, stirring occasionally, until soft, 5 to 7 minutes. Return the chicken to the pot along with the green chilies and stock. Increase the heat to high and bring to a boil. Once boiling, reduce the heat to medium-low and simmer for about 1 hour, or until the chicken begins to fall apart. Remove from the heat, discard the bay leaf, and shred the chicken apart using two forks. Set the shredded chicken meat aside. Extra chicken can be frozen. Place the chicken in freezer bags or airtight freezer containers and freeze for up to four months.

Corn is considered one of the most important staple foods grown by Native Americans.

GOLDEN CHICKEN TAMALES

GREEN CHILI CHICKEN POZOLE

This pozole, a traditional Pueblo stew made with meat and hominy, is one of my go-to dishes for summer parties and outdoor get-togethers. It might sound strange to bring soup to a barbecue, but stewed chicken, fresh herbs, smoky roasted green chilies, sweet hominy, and the spicy crunch of radish are just what a gathering with friends calls for. To be fair, traditional pozole doesn't include roasted green chilies—but to me, they're the make-or-break ingredient to this dish. Their season peaks in August and September, and I roast the chilies myself; that's the flavor people can't stop talking about. If you want to substitute the chicken, try pork, rabbit, bison, or even seafood—scallops, shrimp, and white fish are all delicious substitutions for a fresh take on a traditional dish.

Serves 6 to 8

3 tablespoons canola oil

4 boneless skinless chicken thighs, chopped into small pieces

Salt and freshly cracked black pepper

1 medium onion, peeled and diced

2 stalks celery

2 bay leaves

4 sprigs fresh thyme

2 teaspoons ground cumin

2 teaspoons ground coriander

2 cups (300 g) roasted green chilies (see page 32), diced

4 cups (680 g) cooked hominy (canned is okay), rinsed well

2 quarts (2 L) chicken stock, or as needed

½ cup (60 g) sliced radish, optional

½ cup (30 g) chopped scallions, green part only

In a cast-iron pan or Dutch oven over high heat, add the oil. Season the chicken with salt and pepper. Cooking in batches, add the chicken to the hot oil. Sear on all sides until crusted. Remove the chicken and set aside. Lower the heat to medium-low and add the onion, celery, bay leaves, thyme, cumin, coriander, and green chilies. Sauté, stirring occasionally, until the vegetables are soft, about 10 minutes. Note: If the vegetables get too dry and begin to burn, deglaze the pan with ½ cup (120 ml) water, scraping the bottom of the pan to release any bits. Return the chicken to the pan and add the hominy. Cover the chicken with the chicken stock. Add more stock if necessary. Increase the heat to high and bring to a boil. Remove from the heat and discard the bay leaves and thyme sprigs. Using a slotted spoon, remove 1½ cups (365 g) of the hominy from the pan and transfer to a blender (caution: the hominy will be hot). Carefully puree the hominy until fine and smooth, about 5 minutes. Return the blended hominy to the pan. Reduce the heat to low and allow to simmer for 20 to 30 minutes. Adjust the seasoning if necessary and serve immediately, garnished with the radish, if using, and scallions.

SAGUARO SEED–CRUSTED CHICKEN THIGHS

This recipe, which I created for an event in Phoenix, is a celebration of the desert, the cactus, and the Tohono O'odham, who've inhabited what are now Arizona and Mexico for thousands of years, and whose recipes depend on what grows wild in the desert. It's one of my favorite ways to show how traditional ingredients can meet modern tastes and techniques. Mexican oregano plays a big role here, with its citrusy, slightly licorice flavor. Nutty, crunchy saguaro cactus seeds create a delicious, unique crust for the crispy chicken. And a glaze made with tequila, lime, and agave highlights how other local plants contribute to regional cuisine. Use saguaro cactus seeds in any recipe that calls for poppy seeds; you'll get to try something new and honor the cactus that's one of the defining features of the Sonoran Desert. Its seeds and strawberry-tasting fruit are a staple (and a treat) for the Indigenous people who live in the region.

Serves 6

3 tablespoons canola oil

1 cup (125 g) all-purpose flour

2 eggs, beaten

¾ cup (215 g) saguaro seeds

6 boneless skinless chicken thighs

2 teaspoons salt

1 teaspoon freshly cracked black pepper

1 shallot, peeled and diced

1 clove garlic, peeled

2 teaspoons dried Mexican oregano

Zest and juice of 2 limes

3 ounces (90 ml) tequila

3 cups (720 ml) chicken stock

3 tablespoons agave nectar

Fresh cilantro leaves, for garnish, optional

Preheat the oven to 350°F (175°C).

In a large sauté pan over high heat, add the oil. While the oil is heating, spread the flour on a large plate. Pour the eggs into a wide bowl. Spread the saguaro seeds on another plate. Season the chicken with the salt and pepper and dredge only one side in the flour, shaking off excess. Next, dip the floured side of the chicken into the eggs and then dredge that side in the seeds to evenly coat. This will form the "crust" on the chicken. Place the chicken coated side down in the hot pan. Sear to form a firm crust, 2 or 3 minutes, while making sure the crust does not burn. Carefully turn the chicken and sear the bottom for 2 or 3 minutes. Remove the chicken and transfer to a baking sheet. Place the pan in the oven and bake for 15 to 20 minutes, or until the internal temperature of the chicken reaches 165°F (75°C).

Return the sauté pan to the stove over low heat. Add the shallot, garlic, oregano, and lime zest and juice. Sauté for about 7 minutes, stirring often. Add the tequila (caution: do not touch or shake the pan when adding the tequila or it will flame). Allow the alcohol to cook off, then add the stock and agave nectar. Increase the heat to medium-low and allow to simmer for 30 minutes, or until stock is reduced by half.

To serve, ladle the sauce on a plate and arrange the chicken on top, crust side up. Garnish with fresh cilantro (if using) and serve immediately.

Tohono O'odham Nation

The Tohono O'odham and their predecessors, the Hohokam, first settled in the Sonoran Desert of what's now Arizona and south to Mexico. Their legends say that the Creator (or Earthmaker) took clay from his chest and rolled it into a ball to make the world. And with clay, he baked people. In this way, the community sees everything on earth as interconnected and delicately balanced. Himdag is the guiding principle, encouraging members to treat one another with respect and to interact with the world in a gracious way.

Labyrinths are also central to the community's beliefs and symbology. Many baskets crafted by the Tohono O'odham feature a figure waiting to enter a circular maze—a symbol that represents the challenges of making decisions through life. The answers are believed to be within you, and what's required is for you to search inside the maze to find them. Finding answers is like finding your way to the center of the labyrinth. These circular and square spiral designs also feature prominently in the community's ceramics, jewelry, and pottery.

The Tohono O'odham new year is celebrated in July, when the saguaro cactus fruit is harvested. The fruit can be ten feet (3 m) in the air, so harvesting can be difficult—and dangerous, given the cactus spines. But inside a saguaro, there's a kind of woody skeleton; once the plant dies, the long rib-like sticks within are perfect harvesting tools for the fruit that grows high on the upstretched arms of fruiting saguaro. Once harvested, the fruit is reduced down into a syrup and used in ceremonies and prayers for the monsoon rains that usually come at the end of summer.

Saguaro fruit is a delectable treat in Tohono O'odham cuisine, as are other foraged foods like nuts, cholla cactus buds, herbs, and prickly pear fruits. The community hunted deer and javelinas, boar-like mammals that live mostly on prickly pears. Tohono O'odham also planted the three sisters: corn, beans, and squash.

THE TOHONO O'ODHAM NEW YEAR IS CELEBRATED IN JULY,
WHEN THE SAGUARO CACTUS FRUIT IS HARVESTED.

STEWED CHICKEN WITH GOLDEN TOMATOES

This recipe is adapted from Native American recipes of the northern Pueblo, an area in what's now the American Southwest, which is home to dozens of different communities. My Navajo grandmother, who lived in southern Colorado, often made these stewed tomatoes with peppers and chicken—and it's a recipe that'll always remind me of her, and that place. This dish is all about fresh flavors, bright colors, and varied textures—not to mention the most tender, delectable chicken you can imagine. The white wine isn't traditional in Native recipes, but it's the trick to enhancing the already delicious ingredients. No need to buy an expensive wine, but always cook with something that's enjoyable to drink.

Serves 6

3 tablespoons canola oil

6 skin-on boneless chicken thighs

Salt and freshly cracked black pepper

1 yellow bell pepper, seeded and diced

½ green bell pepper, seeded and diced

1 New Mexican or Anaheim green chili, seeded and diced

1 small onion, peeled and diced

3 cloves garlic, peeled and minced

4 sprigs fresh thyme

1 bay leaf

4 fresh sage leaves

2 cups (480 ml) dry white wine

4 cups (960 ml) chicken stock

2 golden heirloom tomatoes, diced (or 1 quart/540 g red and golden grape tomatoes)

In a cast-iron pan or Dutch oven over high heat, add the oil. Season the chicken with salt and pepper. Add the chicken to the pan and sear on all sides until browned. Remove the chicken and set aside. To the pan add the bell peppers, green chili, onion, garlic, thyme, bay leaf, and sage. Sauté until the peppers are soft and the onion is translucent, about 5 minutes. Add the wine along with the chicken, stock, and tomatoes. Bring to a boil, then reduce the heat to medium-low, cover, and allow to simmer for 35 minutes, or until the internal temperature of the chicken reaches 165°F (75°C). Adjust the seasoning if necessary, remove the thyme sprigs and bay leaf, and serve the chicken immediately with the sauce spooned over the top.

Potlatches, Powwows, and Other Celebratory Feasts

The joy of sharing food is a central part of every culture's celebrations and holiday traditions. It's always precarious to make generalizations, but while the cuisines of different Indigenous communities may vary, at these events the importance of being together, sharing, remains constant. In each Indigenous celebration I've been honored to attend, sacred cuisines are emphasized. Each time, love, joy, and community were the main ingredients.

As the desert's summer heat fades and fall arrives, the Diné (Navajo) New Year celebration Ghááji' begins with the new moon in October. The longer nights mark a time of transition and reflection. It's a time of year to contemplate the things that you want to build and grow in your life, and it's the season of preparing for winter. I think of the sweet, grassy scent of corn during Ghááji' and how the lined texture of the husk feels beneath my fingers. This is the way Diné assess the firmness of the kernels to know whether the ear should be replanted, ground, roasted, or transformed and preserved as Navajo steam corn.

In the Pacific Northwest, potlatch means "to give" in the Chinook language and regional trade jargon. The host gives gifts to the guests. The more generous the host is, the higher their status grows. Potlatch ceremonies are about the joy of gift-giving, sharing, and celebrating the gift of creation.

Powwows are celebratory traditions common across many regions, hosted by different communities as a time to dance, to connect spiritually—and of course, to eat! The word *powwow* has been adopted from the Algonquian language and Ojibwa dialects spoken from the east coast inland to the Ottawa River Valley, which feeds the Great Lakes. At powwows, people trade, sell beautiful handcrafted wares and food, and swap stories, advice, and gossip. A powwow feels like the biggest family reunion. I love seeing people run to hug each other, crying and laughing as they see old friends, cousins, teachers, and relatives. They might have had dinner together just last week or talked on the phone that morning, but it's a powwow, and somehow the air is charged and everything feels more exciting. Time to grab a frybread and find a good spot to sit to catch up and watch the dancers.

Whatever the occasion, I love preparing food for holidays, life milestones, and ceremonies; it reminds me that there is no end to our cycles of returning, improving, and beginning again. These are paths of hope, like the surety of knowing that the seasons will always change but remain constant as they do. Celebratory events and foods connect us to tradition and spirit, family and friends, laughter and nourishment. All these elements are contained in the flavors and scents of cooking.

On the following pages, I've included a sample menu for a celebratory feast you can prepare with your loved ones. Incorporating various traditions, the recipes' Indigenous ingredients will be a delicious conversation starter for any festive occasion.

Chef Freddie Bitsoie's
Celebratory Feast

SERVES 6 TO 8, FAMILY-STYLE

CHOLLA BUDS WITH PIÑON NUTS AND LIME VINAIGRETTE
(PAGE 68)

SAUTÉED FIDDLEHEADS WITH APPLE
(PAGE 118)

SUMMER CORN AND SQUASH
(PAGE 128)

ROASTED DUCK WITH SUMMER BERRY SAUCE
(PAGE 188)

CEDAR PLANK SOCKEYE SALMON
(PAGE 228)

SUMMER PEACH CRISP
(PAGE 270)

GRILLED DUCK
WITH APPLE AND SAGE

During a weeklong event in Idyllwild, California, where I taught home cooks and culinary professionals the art of Native American cooking, I saved the last day to demonstrate how to best grill a duck. Many traditional Indigenous recipes depended on cooking over an open fire—so I think of grilling as the updated method that echoes the traditional. Duck is fatty, which makes it delicious and moist, but expect the drippings to cause flames. You'll want to quickly sear the duck over high heat to get some

grill marks, then finish it with indirect heat so it'll cook without charring. The recipe I first created that day in Idyllwild used leftover apples and herbs, plus some cinnamon and agave, to complement the sage and salty, robust flavor of the duck. The pairing went over exceptionally well, even with a couple of my most respected colleagues: Shane Plumer and Sean Sherman. I'm passing the recipe on to you in the hopes that you'll also enjoy it—and bring something unexpected to your next neighborhood barbecue.

Serves 6 to 8

¼ cup (9 g) chopped fresh sage leaves

2 tablespoons canola oil

Salt and freshly cracked black pepper

1 teaspoon ground cinnamon

1 tablespoon agave nectar

4 Granny Smith apples, cored and halved

1 whole duck, cut into 8 pieces

Prepare and preheat an outdoor grill to high heat.

In a medium bowl, add the sage, oil, 1 teaspoon salt, 1 teaspoon pepper, the cinnamon, and agave nectar. Stir well to incorporate. Add the apples and toss well to coat. Wrap the macerated apples in a sheet or two of aluminum foil (depending on the foil's thickness) and place on the grill. The apples will take about 40 minutes to cook; prepare the duck while they cook and aim to put the duck on the grill with 20 minutes remaining for the apples.

Liberally season the duck with salt and pepper. Arrange the duck skin side down on the grill and cook for 2 or 3 minutes, or until grill marks appear. Turn over the pieces of duck and move them to indirect heat along with the wrapped apples. Indirect heat is accomplished by turning off some of the burners, if using a gas grill, and cooking over the burners not in use, or moving all the coals to one side of the grill and cooking over the unheated side if using a charcoal barbecue. Cover and grill the duck and apples for 15 to 20 minutes, or until the apples are soft and the duck reaches an internal temperature of 165°F (75°C).

Transfer the duck and apples to a serving platter and cover to keep warm. Alternatively, for those who prefer applesauce, simply dice half of the apples and place them in a small bowl. Place the remaining apples in a food mill or processor and process until smooth. Combine the sauce with the diced apples and serve alongside the warm grilled duck.

ROASTED DUCK WITH
SUMMER BERRY SAUCE

Duck has always been a staple of Native American cuisine, particularly in communities from what's now the American Midwest. Ducks have always been plentiful, and besides that, they're delicious, especially paired with berries or other fruit—like the apples in the recipe on page 186. The classic combination of salty-sweet duck and berries appears regularly on menus nationwide, but most people don't know about its origins as a Native American favorite. Traditional recipes would have also included the fresh herbs and cedar needles I've used in this recipe—but not a sauce. That's my contemporary take. Feel free to substitute whatever berries are ripe and in season, or are your favorites. I love duck with blueberries, served with wild rice as the Ojibwa would have (see page 124). A note about the drippings: make sure to use a deep roasting pan; ducks are fatty, and you want to avoid a dangerous spill or sudden splatter.

Serves 6 to 8

1 whole duck

1 small onion, peeled and halved

1 carrot, halved

1 stalk celery, halved

1 tablespoon salt

1 tablespoon freshly cracked black pepper

1 tablespoon dried sage leaves

1 tablespoon dried thyme

½ teaspoon chopped cedar needles, optional

Summer Berry Sauce, recipe follows

Preheat the oven to 350°F (175°C).

In a large roasting pan with rack, place the duck on the rack. Stuff the cavity with the onion, carrot, and celery. Season the duck all over with the salt, pepper, sage, thyme, and cedar needles (if using). Truss the duck with butcher's twine (see page 168). Place the duck in the oven and roast for 1½ hours, or until the internal temperature of the duck reaches 165°F (75°C). Use a meat thermometer to check right where the leg connects to the body. Remove from the oven and serve with summer berry sauce.

SUMMER BERRY SAUCE
Makes approximately 1½ cups (360 ml)

½ cup (70 g) blackberries

½ cup (60 g) raspberries

1 cup (145 g) blueberries

1 cup (145 g) strawberries

½ cup (120 ml) agave nectar

½ teaspoon ground cumin

1 whole clove

1 cup (240 ml) cranberry juice

In a medium saucepot over low heat, add the berries, agave nectar, cumin, clove, and cranberry juice. Stir well to incorporate. Allow to simmer, stirring occasionally, until the sauce thickens, 10 to 15 minutes. Remove from the heat and serve warm with the roasted duck.

WHOLE DUCK WITH JUNIPER BERRIES

There are a lot of ways to cook a duck, but this recipe is special, created from what I've studied about the cuisine of more than twenty early Native American communities in what's now Mississippi. Ducks were abundant in autumn and are often featured in dishes with juniper berries, which grow wild in the region. I've mentioned that ducks are fatty, which is what makes them so flavorful—but there's always the issue of how to render the fat while keeping the meat tender. One effective method, used here, is to simmer your duck in a hot bath, along with fresh herbs, berries, and vegetables. Think of it like making stock as you cook your duck. You're not making soup, though; you'll use the broth and vegetables to create a puree that reflects the richness of the duck fat, earthiness of the root vegetables, and the slight essence of pine from the berries. Don't skip the juniper—it's the small detail that makes all the difference. Try this dish with my Manoomin Rice Salad with Apple-Honey Vinaigrette (page 82), and in one meal you'll capture the entire essence of fall.

Serves 6 to 8

1 whole duck

3 carrots, halved

3 stalks celery, halved

1 large onion, peeled and halved

8 juniper berries

5 sprigs fresh thyme

Salt and freshly cracked black pepper

Juniper branches, washed and snipped into small pieces, for garnish, optional

In a large stockpot, add the duck, carrots, celery, onion, juniper berries, and thyme. Pour 4 to 6 quarts (3.8 to 5.7 L) water over the duck and vegetables, just enough to cover. Turn the heat to medium and bring to a simmer. Cook for 90 minutes, or until the internal temperature of the duck reaches 165°F (75°C), skimming any fat or residue from the surface every 15 to 20 minutes. If the water gets low, add more, just to cover the ingredients. Carefully remove the duck from the pot. Note: Try to keep the duck intact for presentation purposes. Set aside. Remove one halved carrot, one halved celery, and both halves of the onion and place them in a blender along with 4 cups (960 ml) of the broth (skim any fat from the liquid). Puree for 5 minutes, or until velvety smooth. Arrange the duck on a serving platter, drizzle the sauce over and around the duck, and garnish with some juniper branches (if using) just before serving.

BRAISED LAMB SHANKS WITH NAVAJO STEAM CORN

Lamb is common in Hopi and Navajo culinary traditions, and the addition of dried steam corn is what makes this dish uniquely Native American. Luckily Navajo steam corn is easy to order online, as making it is no simple task: you fill an adobe oven with fresh corn on the cob, then seal it with mud and rock. The corn steams all night, and the next day the kernels are dry, ready to be scraped from the ears and dried in the sun. It's a preservation method that lends a smoky-sweet flavor to the corn, to be included in stews or, as in this case, braising liquid. Navajo steam corn pairs beautifully with lamb—that's another thing my grandmother taught me. Whenever a lamb was butchered on her property, the meat would be sliced thin and grilled that evening or made into a delectable soup the following day. My grandmother often requested the shank—an affordable but tough cut of meat. In her hands, with this recipe, it would end up falling-off-the-bone tender, fragrant with fresh herbs and a hint of fresh corn, no matter the season. She'd serve this dish with pan-fried potatoes. It's also delicious over Summer Squash Mash (page 130) or my Sunchoke and Potato Puree (page 131).

Serves 6 to 8

¼ cup (60 ml) canola oil

6 lamb shanks

Salt and freshly cracked black pepper

3 stems fresh rosemary

3 sprigs fresh thyme

¼ cup (35 g) dried and ground Navajo steam corn

1 bunch scallions, white and green parts chopped separately

2 carrots, halved

2 stalks celery, halved

2 tablespoons tomato paste

1 cup (240 ml) dry red wine, optional

5 cups (1.2 L) vegetable stock, or as needed

Preheat the oven to 350°F (175°C).

In a Dutch oven over high heat, add the oil. While the oil is heating, season the lamb with a little salt and pepper. Add the lamb to the hot oil (note: you may have to do this in batches). Sear all sides of the lamb. Once browned, remove the lamb and set aside. Turn the heat to low and add the rosemary, thyme, ground corn, white part of the scallions, carrots, celery, tomato paste, 2 teaspoons salt, and 2 teaspoons pepper. Stir well to incorporate the tomato paste, then sweat the vegetables until the onions are caramelized and the ground corn is toasted, about 10 minutes. Add the wine (if using) or 1 cup (240 ml) water to deglaze the pot and stir so the paste is incorporated into the vegetables. Allow the liquid to evaporate completely. Return the lamb to the pot and cover the lamb with the stock, just enough to cover the ingredients. Add more stock if necessary. Increase the heat to high and bring to a boil. Once boiling, remove from the heat, cover, and place in the oven. Braise for 1 hour and 45 minutes to 2 hours.

After 1 hour and 45 minutes to 2 hours, remove the rosemary, thyme sprigs, carrots, and celery. Adjust the seasoning if necessary and serve the lamb immediately with the sauce. Garnish with the green part of the scallions.

LAMB SOUP WITH BLUE CORN DUMPLINGS

Lamb soup with dumplings is a traditional Navajo dish, originally cooked over an open flame. Now it's often prepared over a wood-burning stove, but a modern stovetop works just as well. This is one of those cozy, filling, comfort-food dishes that's simple to make and impossible to resist. Thick, fragrant stew is peppered with soft, fluffy dumplings that flavor the meaty broth with a hint of fresh corn. This dish appears in this section rather than the Soups chapter because it's always served as a main dish, not a starter course. To make your dumplings the traditional way, never roll them into balls. They're more noodle-shaped: strips of dough cut into pieces. I use blue corn for this recipe since it's both beautiful and traditional, but you can easily swap this for yellow cornmeal if you prefer. You can also substitute sunchokes for the potatoes if you like. Potatoes aren't a traditional ingredient, and neither is the flour in this recipe, but I love how they help thicken the rich, aromatic broth and add to the hearty, rustic experience of the dish.

Serves 6 to 8

2 pounds (910 g) lamb leg meat, cubed

1 tablespoon salt

1 tablespoon freshly cracked black pepper

2 bunches scallions, white parts only

4 russet potatoes, peeled and diced

4 cups (960 ml) beef stock

Blue Corn Dumplings, recipe follows

In a large pot, add the lamb and 4 cups (960 ml) water. Bring to a boil over medium heat. Add 1 tablespoon salt, the pepper, scallions, and potatoes and cook, skimming any impurities from the surface, until the potatoes are fork-tender, 20 to 25 minutes. Add the stock and blue corn dumplings. Continue to cook until the dumplings are firm, about 10 minutes. Remove from the heat and serve.

BLUE CORN DUMPLINGS
Makes about 30 dumplings

1 cup (125 g) all-purpose flour

½ cup (60 g) blue cornmeal

½ teaspoon salt

In a medium bowl, add the flour, cornmeal, and ½ teaspoon salt. Stir until well incorporated. Slowly add 2 cups (480 ml) water while stirring (note: you may not use all the water; this depends on how humid the air is where you're cooking). Once the mixture turns into a dough, remove from the bowl and knead until a smooth ball is formed. Place the dough back into the bowl and cover with a kitchen towel for 15 minutes. To form the dumplings, roll out the dough on a floured surface as thin as you can. Then using a knife or pizza cutter, slice the dough into thin strips, about ½ inch (12 mm) wide and 3 inches (7.5 cm) long. Set the pieces aside until ready to use.

While it's an ancient Navajo tradition to use lamb in soups and stews, classic Indigenous lamb recipes don't call for tomatoes. The two are commonly paired in Mediterranean recipes, though, and it's a combination I love. So I created this soup, intended to be served as a meaty main course, as a way to both honor and modernize my own culinary traditions. I also love that it showcases the bright sweetness of summer tomatoes and garden-fresh zucchini. When I first mentioned the recipe to my grandmother, she was skeptical, but now, this light, brothy soup is one of her seasonal favorites. It's fresh but filling and wonderfully aromatic. Of course, this dish is at its absolute best in late summer, when heirloom tomatoes are at their peak and zucchini is still in season.

Serves 6 to 8

1 to 1½ pounds (455 to 680 g) heirloom tomatoes

2 pounds (910 g) lamb leg meat, cubed

1 stem fresh rosemary

1 medium onion, peeled, halved, and wrapped in cheesecloth

1 tablespoon salt

1 tablespoon freshly cracked black pepper

4 cups (960 ml) beef stock, or as needed

5 cups (575 g) sliced zucchini

3 tablespoons chopped fresh rosemary, for garnish

Bring a pot of water to a boil. Using a paring knife, slice an X on the bottom of each tomato (the side opposite the stem). Fill a bowl with ice and water and set aside. Place the tomatoes in the boiling water for about 40 seconds. Remove the tomatoes and immediately plunge them in the ice water. The edges where the X was scored should start to roll back, allowing the skin to easily be peeled off. Once peeled, core and dice each tomato and set aside.

In a large pot, add the lamb, rosemary stem, and onion. Add enough water to cover the lamb. Bring to a boil over medium heat, then reduce the heat to medium-low, cover, and allow to simmer for 35 minutes. While the lamb is simmering, skim any particles and foam that collect at the surface. Next, add the tomatoes, salt, and pepper and cover with the stock. Add more stock to cover if necessary. Simmer for another 20 minutes. Add the zucchini and simmer for an additional 15 minutes. Remove the rosemary and onion, discarding only the rosemary. Dice the onion and set aside. Add water to the pot if necessary; the soup should have enough liquid that the lamb and vegetables are covered. Adjust the seasoning if necessary. Remove the soup from the heat and serve immediately with the diced onion, garnished with the chopped rosemary.

SUMAC NAVAJO LEG OF LAMB
WITH ONION SAUCE

The Navajo Nation, an area spanning portions of what's now Arizona, New Mexico, and Utah, is the size of West Virginia. At last count, it had a population of around 175,000 people, some of whom still live in traditional log homes called hogans, and some of whom still raise Navajo-Churro sheep—just as they have since the 1500s, when lambs first began showing up in Native recipes. In contrast to some of the dishes in this book, which have been enjoyed by Native Americans for thousands of years, lamb—a centuries-old tradition—is a relatively new addition. Heritage Belle Farms and Dot Ranch are great resources for range-fed, antibiotic-free, parasite-free Navajo-Churro lamb; shop there if you want to keep this recipe as close to authentic as possible. I love this dish as an equally delicious alternative for any roast meat, or any of the braised or stewed lamb dishes in this book. The fragrant, tangy sumac rub perfectly complements the lamb's bold flavor, and the juniper-spiced, herbaceous onion sauce is sure to make this dish a fall and winter favorite. Note: When purchasing a lamb roast, it may be previously tied by the butcher, or left untied. Either will work for this recipe.

Serves 6 to 8

1 cup (95 g) sumac powder

1 teaspoon salt

1 teaspoon freshly cracked black pepper

1 (3-pound/1.4 kg) leg of lamb (or lamb roast)

3 tablespoons canola oil

Onion Sauce, recipe follows

Preheat the oven to 350°F (175°C).

In a small bowl, add the sumac, 1 teaspoon salt, and 1 teaspoon pepper and stir thoroughly to make a rub. Coat the lamb liberally on all sides with the rub. In a large sauté pan over high heat, add 3 tablespoons oil. When the oil is hot, add the lamb and sear on all sides until brown. Transfer the lamb to a baking sheet. Place in the oven and roast for about 35 minutes, or until the internal temperature of the lamb reaches 145°F (65°C) for medium-rare. Remove the lamb from the oven and allow to rest for about 10 minutes before carving. Serve with the onion sauce.

ONION SAUCE
Makes approximately 1½ cups (360 ml)

2 tablespoons canola oil

1 large yellow onion, peeled and julienned

2 sprigs fresh thyme

1 stem fresh rosemary

4 juniper berries

1 teaspoon salt

1 teaspoon freshly cracked black pepper

2 cups (480 ml) chicken stock

In a medium sauté pan, add 2 tablespoons oil, onion, thyme, rosemary, juniper berries, 1 teaspoon salt, and 1 teaspoon pepper. Turn the heat to medium and sauté until the onion is soft and brown, about 20 minutes, stirring often to make sure the onion and herbs don't burn. Add water if needed to deglaze the pan. Add the stock and allow to simmer until the liquid has reduced by half and the sauce has thickened, about 10 minutes. Remove from the heat and discard the thyme sprigs, rosemary, and juniper berries. Set aside until ready to use.

Navajo

The Navajo (Diné) are from what is now called New Mexico, Arizona, and Utah. Our language is related to the Athabaskan linguistic family, which branches northwest to California's Bay Area, stretching all the way to Alaskan Indigenous communities.

When I introduce myself traditionally for formal events, I say I am Diné (Navajo) of the Tábąąhá Edgewater Clan born for my father's clan, the Nát'oh dine'é Táchii'nii; my maternal grandfather's clan are the Tł'ááshchí'í Red Bottom People, and my paternal grandfather's are the Tsi'naajinii Black Streak Wood People.

The word Navajo comes from the Tewa word navahu'u, which Spanish chroniclers called my ancestors who farmed in valleys. When I say I am Navajo Diné, it's more specific. Translating this helps because dih means up and néh means down, so Diné really means that we, as humans, are the sacred confluence of two surfaces meeting. Where the sky and the earth meet, you will find the Diné are there.

In Diné culture, everything is based on the sacred number four. There are four seasons, four cardinal directions, and four affirmations: dawn to the east and bright white is for thinking; daytime to the south and thoughtful turquoise is for planning; dusk is to the west and shimmering yellow abalone sunbeams for life; and nighttime's meditative black is to the north for hope and faith.

Central to Diné philosophy is that our ability to think as five-fingered beings gives us the power to choose whether we create or destroy. There are many stories about the mythology of Coyote and how Coyote chooses many times to be selfish, and how that plays out. As humans, we all have great strength in our choices. Our thoughts impact our spirituality, life opportunities, and even our physical health. Our thoughts are what make us who we are.

Another important part of my Navajo heritage is our food culture, which is being reclaimed. Not only am I a strong supporter of this movement, especially in the Arizona desert, but I'm happy to see that our land is now being used again for growing bountiful vegetables and crops like broccoli, peppers, tomatoes, and amaranth, as well as corn, chilies, sweet potatoes, and garlic. Like centuries ago, many Navajo are reconnecting with their culinary past, especially through annual harvests of Indigenous foods; desert ingredients like parsnips, cholla buds, and wild spinach, which are all symbolic to Navajo culture.

THE WORD NAVAJO COMES FROM THE TEWA WORD *NAVAHU'U*,
WHICH SPANISH CHRONICLERS CALLED MY ANCESTORS
WHO FARMED IN VALLEYS.

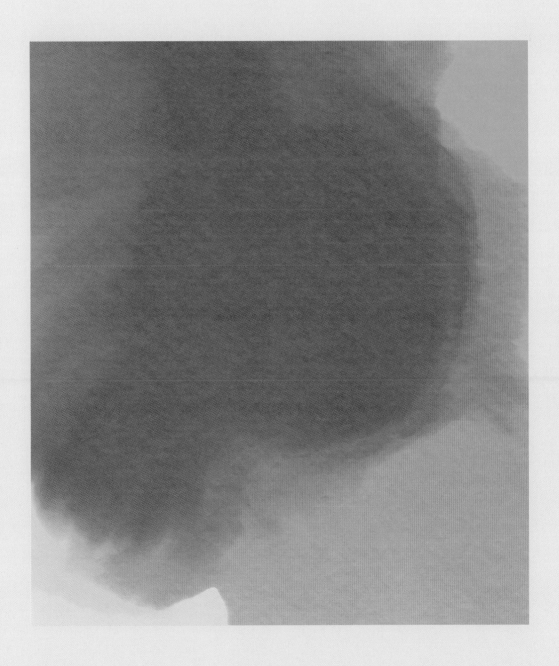

BANANA LEAF AND GINGER-BRAISED PORK SHANKS

Pork isn't a traditional Native American food source; hogs didn't make their way to what's now the continental U.S. until the 1500s—but as the chef for the National Museum of the American Indian in the nation's capital, I've had the pleasure of roasting many pigs for events celebrating Indigenous communities of the Pacific Islands. During those meals, I always try to break away from the kitchen to ask our guests about their secrets to roasting the perfect pig. Traditionally, they'd be roasted whole, underground, in a giant pit. That's just not an option for most people, who don't have the time or space to cook a hundred-pound (45 kg) pig. I've created this crowd-pleasing favorite that features pork shanks wrapped in banana leaves and braised to tender, tasty perfection. This recipe stays true to traditional, time-honored flavors if not entirely to technique. I serve this truly delectable, salty-sweet, ginger-spiced pork with rice, which complements the dish and also honors island traditions.

Serves 4 to 6

4 banana leaves

⅓ cup (75 ml) canola oil

6 pork shanks

Salt and freshly cracked black pepper

1 large onion, peeled and diced

3 plantains, peeled and cut to 4-inch (10 cm) lengths

4 sprigs fresh thyme

2 bay leaves

3 cloves garlic, peeled and minced

1 tablespoon freshly grated ginger

2 teaspoons ground cumin

2 teaspoons ground coriander

2 tablespoons paprika

1 cup (240 ml) orange juice

4 cups (960 ml) chicken stock

Preheat the oven to 350°F (175°C).

Line a Dutch oven with the banana leaves and set aside.

In a large pot over high heat, add the oil. While the oil is heating, season the pork shanks with salt and pepper. Working in batches, sear the pork on all sides until browned. Place all the seared pork in the pot and lower the heat to medium. Add the onion, plantains, thyme, bay leaves, garlic, ginger, cumin, coriander, and paprika. Sweat the onions, stirring occasionally, until soft, about 10 minutes. Deglaze the pot with the orange juice, then add the stock and bring to a boil. Remove from the heat. Transfer the pork to the banana leaf–lined Dutch oven. Pour all the contents from the pot into the Dutch oven and over the pork. Cover and place in the oven. Braise for 1 hour and 45 minutes.

After 1 hour and 45 minutes, remove and discard the bay leaves and thyme sprigs. Transfer the pork to a serving platter or tray using a couple of large spatulas. Cover with the sauce and vegetables. Adjust the seasoning if necessary and serve immediately.

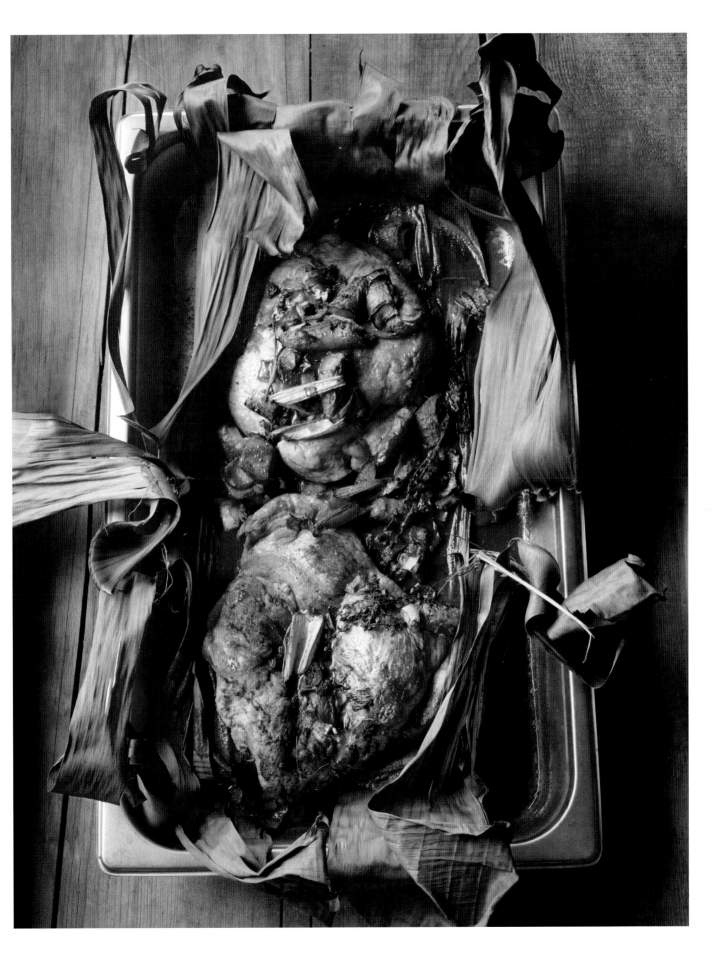

GRILLED PORK LOIN WITH AGAVE GLAZE AND ROASTED TURNIPS

Not long ago, I took part in an agave roast at the Desert Botanical Garden in Phoenix, where a member of the San Carlos Apache community demonstrated the ancient, labor-intensive practice of roasting cactus in an underground, rock-lined oven to extract its natural sweetness. Before he introduced me to agave as a sweetener, I didn't use it much in my recipes; I always reached for honey instead. Now I know that any time a recipe calls for honey, I can use agave. For me, it's a way to honor the cactus of the Sonoran Desert, as well as the traditions of the people who live there. I created this agave glaze to accompany grilled pork, which I absolutely love. The smoky barbecue aromas infuse the salty, spicy meat, and the agave glaze sweetens it just slightly. I like this dish alongside turnips, which caramelize to crispy-sweet tenderness when roasted—they're heaven with the agave glaze. Be sure to start your turnips in advance of the pork, since they'll take much longer to cook.

Serves 4 to 6

2 tablespoons salt

2 tablespoons freshly cracked black pepper

1 tablespoon chili powder

½ cup (120 ml) canola oil

1 (1¼-pound/1 kg) pork loin

Agave Glaze, recipe follows

Fresh flat-leaf parsley, for garnish

Roasted Turnips, recipe follows

In a medium bowl, add 2 tablespoons salt, 2 tablespoons pepper, chili powder, and oil and stir well to combine. Add the pork, making sure it's well covered in the marinade. Place in the refrigerator for 4 hours. Let rest at room temperature for 1 hour prior to grilling.

When ready to grill, prepare an outdoor grill or barbecue to high heat. When hot, arrange the marinated pork on the grill and sear each side for 4 minutes, or until grill marks appear. Lower the heat to medium (if using a gas grill) or carefully move the coals to one side and shift the pork to the other (unheated) side without the coals and cook over indirect heat (if using a barbecue), covered, for 6 minutes, or until the internal temperature of the pork reaches 145°F (65°C). Remove from the heat, brush with agave glaze, garnish with parsley, and serve immediately with roasted turnips.

AGAVE GLAZE
Makes approximately 3 cups (720 ml)

4 cups (960 ml) agave nectar

2 tablespoons brown sugar

½ teaspoon vanilla extract

2 whole cloves

1 teaspoon salt

1 teaspoon freshly cracked black pepper

In a small saucepot over low heat, add the agave nectar, brown sugar, vanilla, cloves, 1 teaspoon salt, and 1 teaspoon pepper. Stir well to combine. Continue to stir until the agave nectar reduces to approximately 3 cups (720 ml). Be careful not to burn the glaze. Remove from the heat and keep warm until ready to serve. Remove the cloves before brushing the glaze onto the pork.

ROASTED TURNIPS
Serves 6

2 tablespoons canola oil

2 teaspoons Mexican oregano

1 teaspoon salt

1 teaspoon freshly cracked black pepper

2 or 3 large turnips (about 1 pound/455 g total), diced

1 small onion, peeled and julienned

In a large bowl, add the oil, oregano, salt, and pepper. Stir well to combine and then add the turnips and onion, tossing well to coat. Transfer the seasoned turnips in equal portions to six individual sheets of aluminum foil so each guest has their own packet of roasted turnips. Divide the onion among the six sheets of foil. Wrap up the foil packets.

Prepare an outdoor grill or barbecue to medium heat. If using a gas grill, set to medium. If using a charcoal barbecue, carefully move the ash-covered coals to one side and leave the other (unheated) side vacant for indirect cooking.

Arrange the foil packets on the grill (indirect side if using a charcoal barbecue). Cover and roast the turnips until fork-tender, 30 to 40 minutes. Remove from the heat and set aside.

Turnips are root
vegetables commonly grown
in temperate climates.

GRILLED PORK LOIN WITH AGAVE
GLAZE AND ROASTED TURNIPS

Apache

The Apache were traditionally nomadic in the Southwest region including Texas, New Mexico, Arizona, Colorado, and northern Mexico. The name *Apache* has Spanish origins, but it has been adopted as the name uniting this group of many communities.

One of the most well-known Chiricahua Apache members is Geronimo, who was lauded for his abilities as a spiritual healer. Those who knew him said that he healed the sick and could slow time, that he could summon the rain in a drought and could see into the future.

Numerous Apache traditions revolve around hunting and honoring the life of the buffalo, deer, and other animals that sustain them. In addition to hunting for food, traditional Apache communities grew corn, sunflowers, beans, and squash. And these traditions continue even now.

One of their most important spiritual ceremonies, passed down through the generations, is the Apache Sunrise Ceremony, or Na'ii'ees: a rite of passage in which girls wear white buckskin dresses, receive their traditional names, and are ushered into adulthood as changing women. Because the number four is sacred, the Sunrise Ceremony lasts for four arduous days; there are prayers, songs, ecstatic dancing, and athletic challenges like running four laps from a tipi to a traditional basket. These kinds of activities are meant to push participants to break free of whatever limits them, shedding preconceptions before they venture into their new roles in the community.

The number four shows up repeatedly throughout the ceremony, in dances and prayers invoking the metaphor of four seasons, four cardinal directions, and four stages of life: infancy, childhood, adulthood, and elderly wisdom. In the final stage of the event, the girl is covered in blessed pollen to reenact the story of the first Apache woman. When she wipes the clay and pollen away, she is reborn a woman.

There's a lot of work to prepare for the ceremony; the family hosting Na'ii'ees gives gifts to all the guests, and of course prepares a feast of traditional food.

NUMEROUS APACHE TRADITIONS REVOLVE AROUND
HUNTING AND HONORING THE LIFE OF THE BUFFALO, DEER, AND
OTHER ANIMALS THAT SUSTAIN THEM.

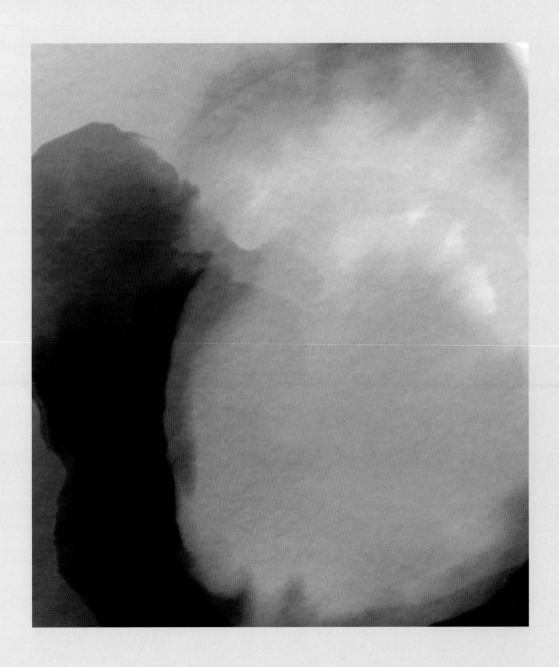

PORK CHOPS WITH CARAMELIZED ONION AND PRICKLY PEAR SAUCE

The traditional Indigenous ingredients in this dish are the prickly pear and onions. This combination creates a deliciously sweet and earthy accompaniment to the saltiness of the pork—a food that was introduced to Native American cuisine thousands of years later. I've spoken earlier in this book about the prickly pear cactus of the Sonoran Desert, which bears a fruit that tastes like a hybrid melon-berry reminiscent of a slightly savory plum, as I hope you will start to experiment with this special ingredient in your kitchen, if you haven't tried it before. Prickly pear blossoms adorn the tops of the cacti's spiny paddles through spring and early summer. The elegant combination of these ingredients creates a simple but impressive dish, ideal for dinner parties or weekend meals year-round. Substitute prickly pear nectar if you can't find organic prickly pear juice; just skip the agave nectar and brown sugar. Serve with Steamed Manoomin Rice with Thyme (page 122); its earthy flavors really come to life alongside fruit-glazed pork chops.

Serves 4 to 6

¼ cup (60 ml) canola oil

6 (6- to 8-ounce/170 to 225 g) pork chops

Salt and freshly cracked black pepper

1 medium onion, peeled and julienned

1 clove garlic, peeled and minced

2 whole cloves

Prickly Pear Sauce, recipe follows

2 grapefruits, cut into supremes, for garnish, see Note

Note: To supreme a grapefruit means to remove the flesh from the peel and pith. To accomplish this, first trim the top and bottom of the grapefruit using a sharp knife so the grapefruit can stand on its flat ends. Next, cut lengthwise between the flesh and the peel, following the fruit's contour, to remove both the peel and pith. Once the grapefruit is void of any white pith (you may need to further trim to remove the pith), slice the grapefruit lengthwise between the segments and the membrane until you reach the center of the fruit. Now make a similar slice on the other side of the segment. Use your knife to remove the segment and repeat for the other segments.

Preheat the oven to 350°F (175°C).

In a large sauté pan over high heat, add the oil. Season the pork chops with salt and pepper and add to the pan when the oil is hot. Note: Do not crowd the pan or the chops will steam instead of sear; work in batches if necessary. Sear the chops for 2 to 3 minutes on each side , or until golden brown. Remove the chops from the pan and transfer to a baking sheet. Set aside. Reduce the heat to medium-low and add the onion, garlic, and cloves. Slowly caramelize the onion until golden brown, about 25 minutes. To avoid burning the onion, add a little water to the pan in ¼-cup (60 ml) increments as you cook. While the onions are caramelizing, place the chops in the oven until fully cooked and their internal temperature reaches 165°F (75°C), 20 to 25 minutes.

When the chops and onions are finished cooking, transfer the chops to a serving platter. Remove and discard the cloves. Spoon the onion mixture over the chops along with the prickly pear sauce. Garnish with the grapefruit supremes and serve immediately.

PRICKLY PEAR SAUCE
Makes approximately 2 cups (480 ml)

4 cups (960 ml) prickly pear juice

1 cup (240 ml) agave nectar

½ cup (110 g) packed brown sugar

Zest and juice of 1 lemon

In a medium saucepot over medium heat, add the prickly pear juice, agave nectar, brown sugar, and lemon zest and juice. Bring to a boil while stirring frequently. Reduce the heat to low and simmer until the liquid is reduced by half. Remove from the heat and serve over the pork chops.

PORK CHOPS WITH CARAMELIZED ONION
AND PRICKLY PEAR SAUCE

Picking prickly pears in
Arizona's Sonoran Desert

SPICE-RUBBED
PORK TENDERLOIN

Recently, I made a culinary sojourn to New Mexico to attend a daylong pork roast with one of the many Pueblo communities in the area. For all Native Americans, food, feasts, and ceremony are interconnected—so I was honored to be invited. There, I discovered a way to season pork based on a Pueblo recipe dating back nearly five hundred years. Pork tenderloin is a common enough dish; you've probably tried it many times. But I suspect you haven't tried it with the Pueblos' own infusion of spices, which has become one of my favorite preparations. A little sweet, a little spice, a little smoke, and a little sage make this recipe one to return to again and again. Serve it warm or cold, in any season, paired with any of the salads, vegetables, or starches in this book. It's incredibly versatile, and incredibly delicious.

Serves 4 to 6

1 teaspoon cayenne pepper

2 tablespoons chili powder

2 tablespoons ground cumin

1 teaspoon salt

1 teaspoon brown sugar

½ teaspoon dry mustard

½ teaspoon dried sage leaves

1 pound (455 g) pork tenderloin

3 tablespoons canola oil

Preheat the oven to 350°F (175°C).

In a small bowl, add the cayenne, chili powder, cumin, salt, brown sugar, dry mustard, and sage and stir well. Rub the pork liberally with the spice mixture on all sides. In a large sauté pan or griddle over medium-high heat, add the oil. When the oil is hot, sear the pork on all sides until the spices form a crust. Place the pork on a baking sheet. Place in the oven and roast until the internal temperature of the pork reaches 165°F (75°C), 20 to 25 minutes. Remove the pork and set aside to rest for 5 to 10 minutes before carving.

BRAISED RABBIT WITH MUSTARD SAUCE

Prior to the mid-twentieth century, rabbit had been one of the most common game animals in Native American cuisine. They were abundant and available throughout the year, often snared by women and children, whose job it was to hunt them. They were cleaned and cut into sections, washed in cold water, and either roasted, boiled, or added to soups and stews. As time went on and Native cultures were forced to change, game hunting became less common. Rabbit dishes are seeing a new resurgence in Native American recipes, however—particularly with Indigenous people in the plains of northern Texas and southern Oklahoma, where this braised rabbit recipe is thought to originate. The sharp tang of mustard is a modern addition, as are the bacon and white wine—which add both flavor and tenderness. It's true that rabbit can be tough if it's too lean—but after an hour of braising that won't be a concern. You'll end up with a fragrant, rich, one-pot meal scented with rosemary—not to mention the meaty, earthy goodness of fork-tender rabbit.

Serves 4 to 6

½ cup (40 g) chopped bacon

2 tablespoons canola oil

6 rabbit legs

Salt and freshly cracked black pepper

1 medium onion, peeled and diced

1 stem fresh rosemary

1 bay leaf

1 cup (240 ml) dry white wine, optional

2 cups (480 ml) chicken stock

½ cup (120 ml) Dijon mustard

6 stems fresh rosemary or parsley, for garnish

In a large pot over low heat, add the bacon. Render the bacon while making sure it doesn't burn. When fully cooked, remove the bacon and drain on a paper towel–lined plate.

Add the oil to the bacon fat and increase the heat to medium. Season the rabbit with salt and pepper. When the oil is hot, sear the rabbit until browned on all sides. Remove from the pot and set aside. (Note: You may have to sear the rabbit in batches; overcrowding in the pot will lead to steaming and not searing.) Reduce the heat to low and add the onion, 1 stem rosemary, and the bay leaf and stir to incorporate the flavors. Deglaze the pot with the wine (if using) or 1 cup (240 ml) water, scraping up any brown bits. When the onions have softened, about 10 minutes, return the rabbit to the pot and add the stock and mustard. Stir to incorporate. Bring to a boil, then reduce the heat to medium-low.

Cover and allow the rabbit to braise for 40 to 50 minutes, or until the rabbit is fork-tender. Adjust the seasoning if necessary. Remove and discard the bay leaf and rosemary and remove the pot from the heat. Transfer the rabbit to a serving platter. Pour the juices over the top and garnish with fresh rosemary or parsley stems just before serving.

GRILLED RABBIT WITH PRICKLY PEAR BARBECUE SAUCE

I've already mentioned that rabbits have been a staple of Native American cooking for centuries, but they don't always get the culinary recognition they deserve. The taste of rabbit is often likened to chicken, which is only partially true. Rabbit can be prepared in many of the same ways as chicken—you've seen it here with dumplings, braised with wine, seared and roasted with root vegetables. But rabbit has a much more robust flavor: it's earthy, meaty, and less delicate, which means you can really experiment with bold flavors without fear of overpowering the meat. To that end, I've created this spicy, smoky recipe with a squeeze of lime—plus added the modern splashes of tequila and a tangy-sweet prickly pear barbecue sauce for an extra burst of flavor. Your local butcher can always section a rabbit for you, but for the intrepid home cook, I've included a quick tutorial following this recipe.

Serves 6 to 8

1 tablespoon salt

1 tablespoon freshly cracked black pepper

2 teaspoons paprika

½ teaspoon cayenne pepper

Zest and juice of 1 lime

2 ounces (60 ml) tequila

¼ cup (60 ml) canola oil

1 whole rabbit, sectioned into pieces (see page 220)

Prickly Pear Barbecue Sauce, recipe follows

In a medium bowl, add the salt, pepper, paprika, cayenne, lime zest and juice, tequila, and oil. Whisk until well combined. Add the rabbit pieces to the bowl, making sure they are well coated. Refrigerate for about 1 hour.

Prepare and preheat an outdoor grill to high heat.

When the grill is hot, add the rabbit to the grill over direct heat. Sear for 3 minutes, or until grill marks appear. Turn the rabbit over and move to indirect heat. Indirect heat is accomplished by turning off some of the burners if using a gas grill and cooking over the burners not in use, or moving all the coals to one side of the grill and cooking over the unheated side if using a charcoal barbecue. Cover and grill the rabbit for 20 minutes, or until the rabbit reaches an internal temperature of 160°F (70°C). Remove from the heat and toss the rabbit with the prickly pear barbecue sauce before serving.

PRICKLY PEAR BARBECUE SAUCE
Makes approximately 1 cup (240 ml)

1 cup (240 ml) ketchup

½ cup (120 ml) prickly pear juice

¼ cup (55 g) packed brown sugar

1 tablespoon red wine vinegar

1 tablespoon Worcestershire sauce

2 teaspoons dry mustard

½ teaspoon onion powder

¼ teaspoon garlic powder

In a small saucepan over low heat, add the ketchup, prickly pear juice, brown sugar, vinegar, Worcestershire sauce, dry mustard, onion powder, and garlic powder. Whisk to combine and bring to a simmer. Simmer until the sauce has reduced and thickened to barbecue sauce consistency. Remove from the heat and set aside until ready to use.

Sectioning a Rabbit

There are three main parts to a rabbit: forelegs, hind legs, and loin.
The loin can be further broken down into rack, saddle, and bellies.

1 Forelegs

The forelegs of a rabbit are easily separated, as they are connected only by muscle tissue. With the rabbit lying on its side, lift the foreleg and feel the joint. Using a sharp knife, holding the foreleg with your other hand, make a smooth cut along the natural seam under the foreleg, cutting toward the head. Remove the foreleg. Repeat the process on the other foreleg.

2 Hind Legs

With the rabbit flat on its back, cut along the inside seam where the hind leg connects to the loin. Grab the hind leg and bend it in the opposite direction and pop the ball joint out of the socket. Finish removing the leg by cutting from the top of the hind leg toward the tail end of the loin. Repeat on the other leg.

3 & 4 Belly

With the rabbit on its back, cut the belly off following the belly seam along the loin. Once you come to the ribs, you have two options.

Option 1: Cut down the rib cage and remove the belly at the ribs, leaving the rib cage meat.

Option 2: Cut to the rib cage and fillet the meat off the rib cage.

6 & 7 Loin

With the belly, forelegs, and hind legs removed, remove the rib cage. With a pair of heavy-duty kitchen scissors, cut along the rib cage where it connects to the loin. Repeat on the other side and remove the rib cage. With the rib cage removed, you can cut the loin into a rack and a saddle. If you cut the loin in half directly behind the removed rib cage, you will now have a rack section and a saddle section.

RABBIT CUTS

1 Forelegs   6 & 7 Loin

2 Hind Legs   6 Rack

3 & 4 Belly   7 Saddle

5 Rib Cage

SEARED RABBIT LOIN
WITH SUNCHOKES

Here's my take on a dish I've seen on a number of menus in Indigenous restaurants on the East Coast, from New York up to Canada. Rabbit and sunchokes are both traditional Native American ingredients, but the pairing doesn't correspond to any long-standing Indigenous dish and seems to be a recent innovation. It's one I appreciate: the earthiness of rabbit is mellowed by the nuttiness of sunchokes, and both are especially delicious with this tarragon sauce I created to lend a hint of springtime and freshness to the rustic flavors. My recipe calls only for the rabbit loin because it's lean, tender, and affordable—though traditionally any Indigenous recipe would use the whole animal. As always, find meat that's antibiotic- and hormone-free and use the fresh loins within a few days of purchase. If you're using frozen loins, use them within a day or two of thawing.

Serves 4 to 6

3 tablespoons canola oil

3 (8-ounce/225 g) boneless rabbit loins

Salt and freshly cracked black pepper

Tarragon Sauce, recipe follows

Roasted Sunchokes, recipe follows

Preheat the oven to 350°F (175°C).

In a large sauté pan over high heat, add the oil. Season the rabbit with salt and pepper. When the oil is hot, sear the top side of the loins until nicely browned. Remove from the pan and transfer to a baking sheet, seared side up. Place in the oven and roast for 15 to 20 minutes, or until the internal temperature of the rabbit reaches 160°F (70°C). Transfer the rabbit to a serving platter and pour tarragon sauce over the top. Serve with roasted sunchokes.

TARRAGON SAUCE
Makes approximately 1 cup (240 ml)

½ cup (70 g) diced shallot

5 sprigs fresh tarragon

2 cloves garlic, peeled

1 bay leaf

2 cups (480 ml) chicken stock

½ cup (120 ml) dry white wine, optional

In a small sauté pan over low heat, add the shallot, tarragon, garlic, and bay leaf. Sweat the shallot, stirring occasionally, for about 5 minutes. Deglaze the pan with the stock and wine (if using). Allow to simmer until the liquid is reduced by half. Adjust the seasoning if necessary and remove the garlic, tarragon, and bay leaf before serving.

ROASTED SUNCHOKES
Serves 4 to 6

¼ cup (60 ml) canola oil

1 tablespoon salt

1 tablespoon freshly cracked black pepper

1 teaspoon paprika

1½ pounds (680 g) sunchokes (Jerusalem artichokes), sliced into rounds

2 tablespoons unsalted butter, melted

½ cup (25 g) chopped fresh flat-leaf parsley

Preheat the oven to 350°F (175°C).

In a large bowl, add the oil, salt, pepper, and paprika and stir well to combine. Add the sunchokes and toss well to coat. Line a baking sheet with parchment paper and arrange the seasoned sunchokes on the sheet. Place in the oven and roast until fork-tender, 30 to 35 minutes. Remove from the oven and transfer to a serving bowl. Toss with the melted butter and parsley. Serve immediately.

ROASTED SUNCHOKES

SEARED RABBIT LOIN
WITH SUNCHOKES

ALASKAN KING SALMON
WITH CRUSHED PECANS

This recipe features fresh wild king salmon from Alaska, also known as chinook—one of the most delicious salmon on earth. They're in season from June through August, and highly sought-after by chefs and sport fishermen, as well as Orca whales and sea lions. Unfortunately, due to a combination of factors, their numbers are dwindling. Coho and sockeye are more abundant, and both are delicious substitutes in this recipe: coho will be the milder of the two, and sockeye the most salmon-y of all the salmon—which makes it a favorite for true salmon lovers when conservation is a concern. This recipe appears here as a way to honor the recipes of the Indigenous communities in the Pacific Northwest, what's now British Columbia and Alaska—where, for thousands of years, Indigenous people dried, boiled, and smoked salmon as a staple of their diet. If you live in the Pacific Northwest, many communities along the coast sell wild catch that you can buy directly. Here I've created a recipe that pairs two Indigenous foods from disparate communities— the salmon from the Northwest, and pecans from the Midwest. The sweet crunch of pecans and honey combine with the tang of Dijon mustard to produce a salmon dish fit for any special occasion.

Serves 6

3 tablespoons Dijon mustard

3 tablespoons unsalted butter, melted

1½ tablespoons honey

½ cup (25 g) fresh bread crumbs

½ cup (45 g) finely chopped or crushed pecans

1 tablespoon chopped fresh flat-leaf parsley

6 (4-ounce/115 g) fresh wild-caught Alaskan king salmon fillets

Salt and freshly cracked black pepper

6 lemon wedges

Prepare an outdoor grill to medium heat (if using a gas grill) or carefully move the coals to one side (if using a barbecue). Or preheat the oven to 400°F (205°C).

In a small bowl, add the mustard, melted butter, and honey and stir well to combine. In another bowl, add the bread crumbs, pecans, and parsley and stir well to combine. Season each salmon fillet with salt and pepper. Place the fillets, skin side down, on a greased baking sheet and brush the tops of each fillet liberally with the mustard-honey mixture. Then cover the top of each fillet with the bread crumb–pecan mixture. Place on the grill skin side down, or place the baking sheet in the oven. Cook for about 10 minutes per 1 inch (2.5 cm) of thickness, measured at the thickest part, or until the salmon just flakes when tested with a fork and the internal temperature of the salmon reaches 145°F (65°C). Note: The salmon will continue to cook when removed from the heat, so it's best to slightly undercook. Transfer the fillets to a serving platter or individual plates and serve with the lemon wedges.

CEDAR PLANK SOCKEYE SALMON

As I've mentioned, salmon is at the heart of Native American cuisine in the Pacific Northwest and British Columbia. One of my most memorable experiences of cooking salmon was on North Vancouver Island near Port Hardy, home of the Kwakawaka'wakw people. There, members of the community showed me one of their most sacred traditional recipes: sockeye salmon butterflied open, speared on cedar stakes, and placed near an open fire. As it slowly roasted, the fish absorbed the delicious smoky cedarwood aroma. Sockeye is perfect for the at-home, plank-roasted version of that traditional Kwakawaka'wakw people dish; it has the most intense flavor of any salmon, so it won't be overpowered by the fragrant cedar. If sockeye is a little too fishy for your personal taste, try the milder coho or decadent king. I'd stay away from pink or chum salmon; they're also used widely in traditional Indigenous dishes, but in a recipe where the fish is the focal point, they'll seem bland and soft. You'll see I've replaced the whole fish with salmon fillets, and cedar stakes with planks. If you don't enjoy the scent of cedar, use an untreated plank of alder or applewood instead—it'll still transfer a delicious aromatic quality to your salmon. See page 230 for more tips on cooking with planks.

Serves 4

2 juniper berries, ground

6 fresh sage leaves, chopped

1 teaspoon salt

1 teaspoon freshly cracked black pepper

3 tablespoons canola oil

4 (6-ounce/170 g) wild sockeye salmon fillets

4 cedar planks, soaked in water for 30 minutes

In a medium bowl, add the juniper, sage, salt, pepper, and oil and stir well. Add the salmon fillets, turn to cover, and let marinate in the refrigerator for 4 hours.

When you're ready to cook, preheat an outdoor grill to medium or preheat the oven to 350°F (175°C).

Place each fillet skin side down on a cedar plank and arrange on the grill. Close the lid and grill until the internal temperature of the fillets reaches 145°F (65°C), 10 to 12 minutes. Note: Small fillets will cook quicker than larger cuts. Start checking the salmon for doneness after 10 minutes.

If cooking in the oven, place each fillet skin side down on a cedar plank and arrange on a baking sheet. Place the pan in the oven and cook until the internal temperature of the fillets reaches 145°F (65°C), 10 to 12 minutes.

Remove from the heat and transfer the plank with the fillets to a serving platter or baking sheet. Serve immediately.

Cooking with Wood Planks

In the Pacific Northwest, Native American communities have been cooking with wood planks, particularly alder and cedar, for centuries. Not only does the wood serve as a practical means of securing the food so it doesn't fall into the fire, but the wood is an important tool in the cooking process. As the food, such as salmon, cooks over the flame, the fish absorbs the extra moisture (steam) from the wood, which keeps the flesh from drying out while infusing it with that fragrant and smoky-savory goodness. Today, wood-plank cooking, or simply "planking," remains a technique for a classic regional dish for those looking to infuse their foods as the Native Americans have done. Planking is also a healthy way to cook without using a lot of butter or oil.

Let's talk about the plank itself. For seafoods, including salmon, I prefer cedar, but you can also use alder or applewood. Always make sure the cooking plank is untreated. To avoid any doubt, purchase planks at your local seafood market or grocery store. I find the thicker the plank the better. Planks that are too thin (resembling a roof shingle) will burn and char very easily. Planks that are at least ½ inch (12 mm) thick are my preference. Not only do they warp less while cooking, they are more resilient. You'll often get three or four uses from them before you find yourself breaking apart the blistered wood into chips for your fireplace or for a pleasant smoky addition to your next barbecue. Serving your cooked food, such as a fillet of salmon, directly on the plank also makes for an attractive presentation, which is better accomplished by a thicker plank that didn't burn to a crisp in the process.

Before you arrange that beautiful piece of salmon on your plank, make sure to soak the wood. This keeps the plank from burning too quickly while also keeping the food moist during the cooking process. I soak my cedar or alder planks for at least a couple hours in white wine for extra zest. You can also use water. Just make sure to weigh down your plank so it's not floating. You want to soak the entire plank. Before cooking, I will also "cure" my plank by first placing it on the grill, closing the lid, and heating the wood for a couple minutes on each side. I find this enhances the flavor and prevents the plank from warping when cooking.

Right before planking, I prefer to brush a little oil on the plank. This prevents delicate foods, especially seafood, from sticking. Also, remember that wood conducts heat more slowly than a metal grill, so planked foods will need a little longer to cook. Another helpful hint is to keep the grill's lid closed as much as possible to maintain a steady temperature and maximize smoking. Also, keep a spray bottle filled with water handy so flames can be extinguished if the plank starts to burn. To avoid flare-ups, use indirect heat with the grill closed. Planked food does not have to be turned during grilling, so leave the salmon untouched on the plank during the grilling process. For proteins, such as salmon, the flesh will continue to cook once taken off the heat, so keep that in mind to make sure you do not overcook your fish.

Lastly, planking is not reserved just for outdoor fires and grills. You can easily prepare seafood and other foods on a wood plank for the oven. Simply place the soaked plank on a baking sheet, arrange the food on top, and place in a preheated oven. For salmon, place the fillet skin side down on the plank and bake for 10 to 12 minutes at 350°F (175°C), or until the flesh can be flaked with a fork. The key to cooking salmon is lower heat. If the salmon begins to bubble with a lot of white residue, you're cooking the fish at too high a heat.

Wood cooking planks, like alder and cedar, are available at most seafood markets and grocery stores.

Kwakawaka'wakw

The Kwakawaka'wakw are a group of several communities from what is now British Columbia in Canada. Fish, particularly salmon, has always been a prominent part of the Kwakawaka'wakw cuisine; traditionally, these peoples fished from cedar canoes with nets, harpoons, and fish traps. The tradition of gathering clams, seaweed, and mussels continues today, but of course modern boats are used day to day. Canoes are still common at ceremonies and festivals, however.

The Kwakawaka'wakw made a tradition of smoking their salmon to preserve it, in smokehouses near the beach that still exist today. Another traditional cooking method was steaming: they'd fill a cedar box with water, then add extremely hot rocks to cook the food and infuse it with flavor. The two methods often combined: since fish was traditionally dried to preserve it for the winter stores, steaming was a good way to rehydrate and heat it for winter meals. Their smelt fish and smoked salmon were valuable and sought after; that allowed them to trade with other communities for necessities like Tlingit fabric, blankets, and tapestries and Haida canoes.

The Kwakawaka'wakw didn't eat only seafood; they also traditionally hunted deer, birds, bear, caribou, elk, and moose with bows and arrows and gathered berries, roots, and cedar to use as spices and in teas.

Totem poles are a prominent cultural element among the communities of Canada's west coast. The lower characters on the totem pole are especially revered for their eye-level position and their strength to hold up the spirits above them. Kwakawaka'wakw totem poles depict six figures representing different clans united in an alliance to work together.

I like thinking of this idea of alliance in terms of cooking: there may be one ingredient, like salmon, that you're building around, but other flavors and textures are working together to make something beautiful, delicious, and balanced.

THE KWAKAWAKA'WAKW MADE A TRADITION OF SMOKING
THEIR SALMON TO PRESERVE IT, IN SMOKEHOUSES NEAR THE
BEACH THAT STILL EXIST TODAY.

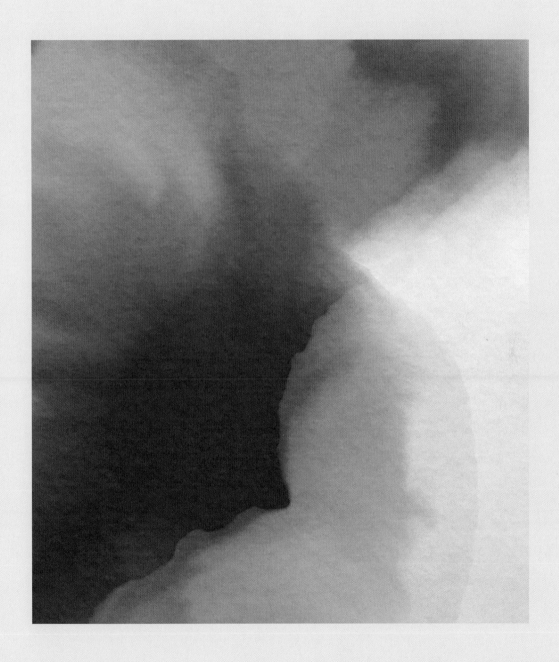

CORNMEAL-CRUSTED WALLEYE WITH ROASTED CORN AND GREEN CHILIES

This recipe features a fish that was savored by many Indigenous communities, from the First Nations of Ontario to the Ojibwe of what's now Michigan, Wisconsin, Minnesota, and North Dakota. Caught during the summer in inland lakes and rivers using traps called weirs, walleye was traditionally hung on racks to cook and dry over a fire. In winter, the fish could be quickly boiled and rehydrated for any number of recipes. My modern version skips the drying and rehydrating; instead, it celebrates the flaky white meat of the fresh fish. Again, I've taken

Indigenous ingredients from another region to round out this recipe—in this case, drawing on the flavors of the Southwest. This light, summery dish is quick to prepare and bursts with the flavors of fresh corn, smoky roasted chilies, and wild mushrooms. If you have to make a choice, use frozen fish and garden-fresh vegetables— their just-picked flavors are tough to replicate out of season. As with all fish, be sure to cook your walleye within a day or two after it's caught or purchased. Frozen walleye can be kept in the freezer for up to a year.

Serves 4

4 ears corn, husks removed

3 tablespoons canola oil

½ cup (60 g) yellow cornmeal

1¾ teaspoons salt

½ teaspoon freshly cracked black pepper

½ teaspoon cayenne pepper, or as needed

4 (6-ounce/170 g) walleye fillets

3 tablespoons unsalted butter

½ pound (225 g) fresh wild mushrooms, sliced

2 roasted green chilies (see page 32), chopped

Preheat the oven to 350°F (175°C).

Brush the corn with 1 tablespoon of the oil. Arrange the corn on a baking sheet and cover with aluminum foil. Roast in the oven for 30 to 40 minutes, or until tender. Remove and let cool. Cut the corn from the cobs.

In a large bowl, add the cornmeal, 1 teaspoon of the salt, the pepper, and cayenne, adjusting the cayenne depending on your desired level of heat. Stir well to combine, then dredge the walleye fillets in the mixture, shaking off excess. In a large skillet over medium heat, add the butter. When the butter is hot, sauté the mushrooms until tender, 4 to 5 minutes. Add the green chilies, corn, and remaining salt and sauté for another 2 or 3 minutes, or until the chilies have softened. Remove from the heat and transfer the contents to a bowl. Set aside. Wipe the pan clean and add the remaining oil. Return to medium heat. When the oil is hot, add the fillets. Sauté for 2 to 3 minutes on each side, or until the fish is golden brown and flakes easily with a fork. Remove from the heat and transfer to a serving platter. Spoon the mushrooms, chilies, and corn over the fillets and serve immediately.

Piscataway and Nanticoke-Lenape

Mitsitam translates to "Let's eat!" in the Piscataway language, a fitting name for the restaurant in the Smithsonian museum where I work, which is in what's now called Washington, D.C., located on the Piscataway and Nanticoke-Lenape Peoples' ancestral land.

The Nanticoke-Lenape were formerly known as the Cherokee Nanticoke-Lenape or the Eastern Nanticoke-Lenape, but in their native language, they call themselves the Lenape. They traditionally lived in wooden longhouses, which were built using young saplings that could be bent as needed, then shielded from the rain and snow with bark shingles.

Chesapeake Bay is a flourishing ecosystem that fostered a rich Indigenous food tradition in the area, with its bountiful supply of fish, waterfowl, and shellfish, as well as hunted game like rabbits, wild turkeys, and deer. Among the foraged foods of the region are berries, nuts, oysters, and crabs. Many of these foods were cooked in clay pots, which were also used for storage.

The Piscataway and Nanticoke-Lenape Peoples are also known to be great agriculturists who grow pumpkins, corn, beans, squash, melons, and tobacco. Their lauded crafts include clay pots, flint knives, and wares decorated with dyed porcupine quills. Among the other prized crafts for traditional trade are muslin, wool, silk, and seed beads. Today, some Piscataway tribal craftspeople paint contemporary artwork on deer hides, but the tradition has its roots in ancient practices.

The Piscataway and Nanticoke-Lenape way has always been to use the entire animal out of respect to the sustenance it provides the community. For example, once deer meat had been roasted or dried to preserve it for later meals, the sinew could be used for archery bows; the hides to insulate homes; the bones fashioned into brushes and other tools. The lack of waste is a show of gratitude.

THE PISCATAWAY AND NANTICOKE-LENAPE WAY HAS ALWAYS
BEEN TO USE THE ENTIRE ANIMAL OUT OF RESPECT TO THE
SUSTENANCE IT PROVIDES THE COMMUNITY.

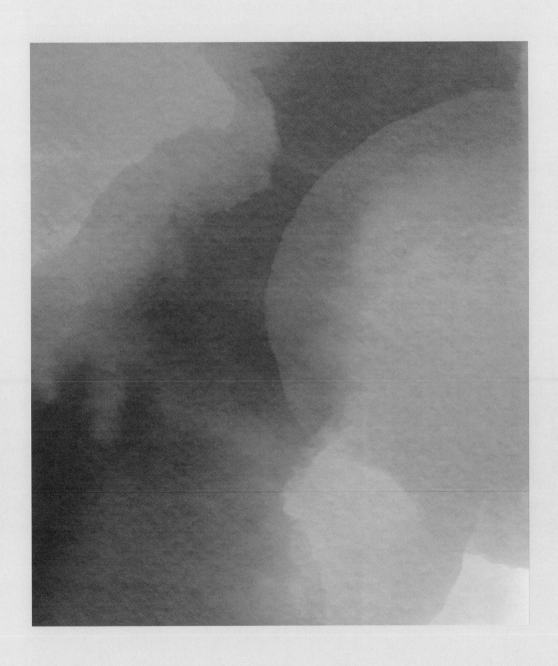

MAKAH CRAB BOIL

Crab have always been a part of the Native American diet, culture, and economy of Pacific Northwest and Alaskan Indigenous communities. This particular crab recipe is based on a tradition of the Makah, who live on the coast of what's now Washington State. I've spent time crabbing with the Makah at Neah Bay and I can wax poetic about Dungeness crab, how their delicate meat tastes as fresh and oceanic as the wind off the water (pages 17 and 72). As you can imagine, this recipe is one of my favorites in this book. The Makah serve crab steamed and roasted too, but this simple, delectable crab boil is my favorite. Make it for one, or make it for twenty; half the fun is in the gathering together to crack your crab (using crab crackers) and savor it dipped in melted butter.

Serves 2

2 tablespoons mustard seed

2 tablespoons celery seed

1 tablespoon dill seed

1 tablespoon coriander seed

1 tablespoon whole allspice

½ teaspoon whole cloves

4 bay leaves

¾ teaspoon salt

¼ cup (60 ml) lemon juice

1 teaspoon cayenne pepper

2 whole live Dungeness crab (2 pounds/
910 g each)

Melted butter and lemon wedges,
for garnish

Lay out a double thickness of cheesecloth, about 6 by 6 inches (15 by 15 cm), on the kitchen counter. In the center, add the mustard seed, celery seed, dill seed, coriander seed, allspice, whole cloves, and bay leaves. Gather the corners of the cloth to enclose the seasonings and tie securely with some kitchen string.

In a large stockpot, add 8 quarts (7.5 L) water, salt, lemon juice, cayenne, and spice bag and bring to a boil over high heat. Using tongs, add the crabs to the pot and return to a boil. Reduce the heat and simmer, covered, until the shells turn bright red, about 18 minutes.

Using tongs, remove the crabs from the pot. Allow to cool until cool enough to handle. Then clean the crabs by removing the top shell and discarding it along with the gills and mandibles (the guts). Rinse the crab clean and serve with the melted butter and lemon wedges.

Makah

The Makah live in what's now northwest Washington State on the Olympic Peninsula. A society intrinsically connected with the sea, the Makah traditionally lived in longhouses: very cozy, single-story rectangular buildings covered in shingles of bark. Ancestral longhouses feel very welcoming, and inside them, you can fall asleep listening to the sound of ocean waves. The name Makah means "generous ones," and was given by neighboring communities; in their own language, the Makah community is called Qwiqwidicciat.

Traditional Makah cuisine features the bountiful salmon and berries of the coast; they also once ate seals and gray whales, which could provide for the village for months. Seal hunters wore their hair in tight buns on top of their heads with burning torches protruding from their hair. This flame torch, dipped in cedar pitch, was a precursor to battery-powered headlamps, and it gave them light to see when they hunted in sea caves.

The Makah's religion is very connected to the sea and whale magic, or cheesum, which is a core part of their identity and culture. Whale hunting expeditions were part of the Makah's ancient ceremonial culture, for which there were extensive rituals of preparation.

In the days before they launched their canoes, fishermen would fast, pray, and bathe ceremonially. Sometimes a hunt would take days. Special songs and prayers accompanied the waves' endless rhythm while the fishermen were out at sea. Makah ancestors taught that to survive, the hunters must become one with the gray whale's spirit and thank it for providing to the community. All the ceremonies were centered on this principle of gratitude and respect.

According to other Makah beliefs, the clever trickster Qweti was the first human. True to their oceanic culture, Qweti was born into the world in a mussel shell and is believed to turn his rivals into small animals that run away. Qweti embodies the friendly, clever, generous spirit of the Makah. Generosity colors all relationships and beliefs among the Makah People, and the elders who have taught me some of their cooking methods were incredibly kind; I'm honored to have shared in their cultural and culinary traditions.

PACIFIC HALIBUT CAKES WITH CAPER MAYONNAISE

Growing up in the Southwest, I was exposed to many red meats and root vegetables, but I didn't develop an affinity for seafood until I began to travel. Exploring different cuisines of Indigenous communities on the east and west coasts of what's now the U.S. and Canada, I immediately understood what I'd been missing. This recipe is a tribute to the flaky, firm, delectable halibut and the dozens of Pacific Northwest communities whose recipes celebrate and depend on it. Try making these cakes with halibut cheeks—it's the most tender and flavorful part of the fish, or substitute crab or any white fish, like cod or tilapia. The capers, mayo, eggs, and panko aren't traditional Native American foods; they're my modern addition to this crispy, delightful dish, which I like to serve as a starter or a light lunch alongside my Swamp Cabbage Salad with Lemon Vinaigrette (page 86).

Serves 4

1 pound (455 g) Pacific halibut, skin removed

Salt and freshly cracked black pepper

2 tablespoons canola oil

½ cup (25 g) minced fresh dill

2 eggs, beaten

⅓ cup (75 ml) mayonnaise

3 tablespoons capers, drained and finely chopped

½ teaspoon cayenne pepper

1 cup (80 g) panko, plus more for coating the cakes

Canola oil, for frying

Unsalted butter

Caper Mayonnaise, recipe follows

Sprinkle the halibut with salt and pepper. In a heavy large skillet over medium-high heat, add 2 tablespoons oil. When the oil is hot, add the halibut and cook until just opaque in the center, about 4 minutes per side. Remove from the heat and transfer to a plate to cool.

Flake the cooled halibut into small pieces and add to a bowl along with the dill, eggs, mayonnaise, capers, cayenne, 1 cup (80 g) panko, and a pinch each of salt and pepper. Gently toss to combine. Place the mixture in the refrigerator for about 15 minutes to cool completely. (Note: It's easier to form the cakes when the mixture is cold.)

Shape the mixture into 3-inch (7.5 cm) diameter cakes, or however large or small you want to make them. The 3-inch (7.5 cm) diameter will make 6 cakes. In a medium bowl, add more panko and coat each cake with the panko, pressing to adhere. When coated, place the cakes back in the refrigerator for 10 minutes to help them set before cooking.

Preheat the oven to 400°F (205°C).

In a large skillet over medium-high heat, add enough oil to cover the bottom of the skillet. Add an equal amount of butter. The amount of oil and butter will depend on the size of your skillet. There should be a fair amount of both in the pan, otherwise the cakes will stick. When the oil and butter are hot, arrange the cakes in the pan and cook for about 1 minute on each side, or until golden brown. Remove from the pan and transfer to a baking sheet. Place in the oven

and allow the cakes to finish cooking, 3 to 5 minutes, or until warmed all the way through. Note: You can keep the cakes warm by turning off the oven and keeping them inside until ready to serve.

Transfer the cakes to plates or a serving platter and serve with caper mayonnaise.

CAPER MAYONNAISE
Makes approximately 1 cup (240 ml)

¼ cup (30 g) capers, drained

¾ cup (180 ml) mayonnaise

1 tablespoon Dijon mustard

1 tablespoon lemon juice

2 tablespoons cold water

1 cup plus 2 tablespoons (270 ml) canola oil

Salt

In a food processor, add the capers, mayonnaise, mustard, lemon juice, and water. Pulse until combined. With the machine on, slowly drizzle in the oil until thickened. Season with salt and serve.

PAN-ROASTED
CUMIN-CRUSTED SABLEFISH

Sablefish, also known as black cod, has mild, white meat that's stunningly smooth and velvety, with large, delicate flakes and a naturally buttery taste. It's been a staple in the recipes of the Lower Elwha Klallam community in what's now northwest Washington State for nearly three thousand years. Because the fish itself is so decadent, I prepare it simply here, with a toasted cumin crust and a light squeeze of lemon.

The cumin isn't traditional, but its warm, earthy fragrance and slightly bittersweet flavor make it the perfect spice to accent the richness of sablefish. This particular fish is more forgiving to the novice cook than most, because the fat acts as a buffer against overcooking. You can tell it's done when it flakes easily. I love this dish alongside my Great Northern Beans with Lemon-Thyme Vinaigrette (page 74).

Serves 4

1 tablespoon cumin seeds

½ teaspoon salt

¼ teaspoon freshly cracked black pepper

4 (6-ounce/170 g) sablefish fillets

Canola oil

½ small onion, peeled and sliced

Lemon wedges and zest, for garnish

Preheat the oven to 375°F (190°C).

In a large ovenproof pan over medium heat, add the cumin seeds and toast for about 2 minutes. Remove the seeds and crush with a kitchen mallet until finely ground. Add to a bowl along with the salt and pepper. Stir well to combine, then rub the sablefish fillets liberally with the cumin mixture.

In the same pan, add enough oil to cover the bottom of the pan. The amount of oil will depend on the size of your pan. Increase the heat to medium-high. When hot, add the cumin-crusted fillets and onion. Sear the fillets until golden brown, about 2 minutes on each side. Remove from the heat and transfer the pan with the fillets and onion to the oven. Bake until the fish flakes easily with a fork, about 5 minutes. Remove from the oven and serve immediately with the pan juices. Garnish with the lemon wedges and zest.

SAUTÉED GARLIC SPOT PRAWNS

You can recognize spot prawns by their white markings: spots on their tails and horizontal bars on the carapace. You can recognize their taste if they're the best prawns you've ever eaten. They're the largest species of shrimp found in the Pacific Northwest, known—and loved—for their firm texture and natural sweetness. Spot prawns are commercially harvested every year by many Indigenous communities, including the Nisqually—but Native-harvested prawns are seasonal and not always easy to find. Buy a pound (or two or three) when you have the chance, and try this delicious, quick, simple recipe in which the bright preserved lemon, earthy garlic, and peppery parsley let the flavor of the prawns shine.

Serves 2 to 4

1½ tablespoons canola oil

1 cup (2 sticks/225 g) unsalted butter, cut into tablespoons

8 cloves garlic, peeled and thinly sliced

¾ cup (40 g) chopped fresh flat-leaf parsley

¾ cup (60 g) sliced preserved lemon

Salt and freshly cracked black pepper

24 fresh whole spot prawns

1 cup (240 ml) dry white wine, optional

Microgreens, for garnish

In a large sauté pan over high heat, add the oil and butter. When the butter is melted, add the garlic, parsley, preserved lemon, salt, and pepper and stir to combine. Cook for several minutes, stirring frequently, making sure not to burn the garlic. Add the wine (if using) or 1 cup (240 ml) water, scraping up any browned bits. Add the spot prawns and sauté until the prawns have turned bright pink, about 2 minutes. Transfer the prawns and pan juices to a serving platter and garnish with the microgreens.

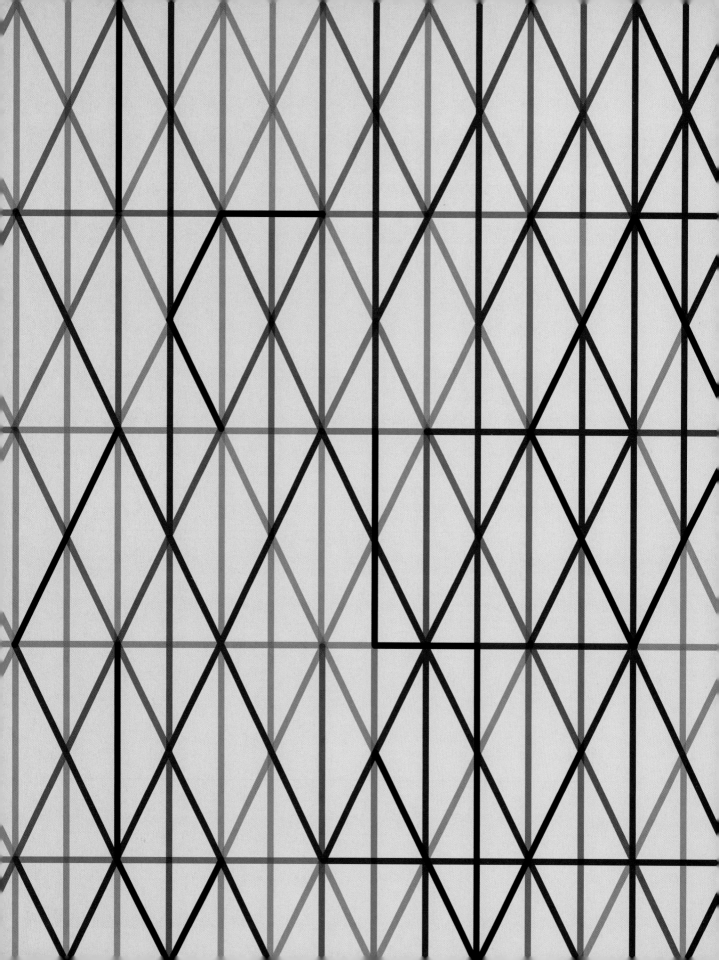

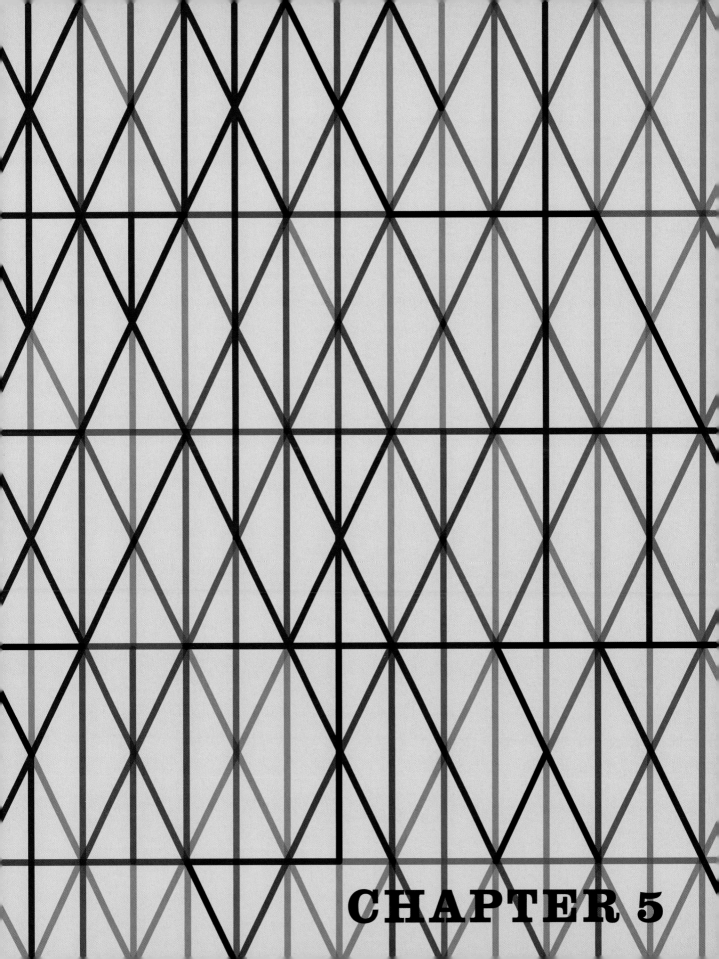

CHAPTER 5

Puddings and Sweets

What I love about these end-of-the-meal treats is that they bring us right back to the beginning of Native American cuisine. There's a misconception that ancestral Indigenous foods were devoid of sweetness altogether, and that sugar entered Native American cuisine only after the arrival of Europeans. But if you think about foods that have grown wild for thousands of years—which I do every day as part of my job—it doesn't take long to come up with plenty of sweet ingredients like agave, prickly pear, fresh fruits, and maple sugar. So I've framed these puddings and sweets around those natural sweeteners and other Indigenous ingredients like pumpkin, corn, nuts, seeds, berries, chocolate, and fresh mint. Of course, the baked goods that require eggs, wheat flour, butter, cream, and refined sugar weren't part of Indigenous food traditions; they're here because sweetness always has been.

Take prickly pears, for example. They're one of my favorite fruits because of their complex, savory sweetness and the astringent pop of acidity in their tiny black seeds. You might think that the phrase "savory sweetness" doesn't make sense. But to me, it's a perfectly natural expression of symmetry and connection. When I look at ceramic Ancestral Pueblo vessels once used by my Navajo ancestors in Chaco Canyon, I think about how they balanced the bitter acidity of chocolate to drink cacao. The cups were made to stack together the same way the flavors do. Every time I create a recipe, I understand that the balance of acid, sweetness, salt, sour, and umami is what will make or break a dessert.

I talk a lot about how a strictly ancestral menu often wouldn't appeal to modern palates, and that definitely applies to the recipes in this final chapter. Look at how many modern dishes incorporate acids, particularly from lemons or limes; that's not something you would've seen a thousand years ago, or even a hundred. Taste preferences change all the time, while for centuries, ingredients themselves have mostly remained constant. Consider the savory desserts that are coming back into fashion.

It's interesting to watch that shift, to see people reject cloying, overly sweet desserts in favor of some spice, bitterness, or acid to balance the sugar.

For me, that seems perfectly natural as well. If you asked me to make you a dish, I'd ask what kind of wine or beer you like, and how much cream you add to your coffee. These defining bitter flavors tell me all the information I need to know about what your favorite foods might be, and how you like them prepared. This is what I mean when I say cooking is a way of communicating. One constant throughout time and culture is that we can speak to each other through food—and these puddings and sweets are no exception.

When we eat sweets, we often do it while gathering to celebrate, so these dishes are made to be shareable. My intention is to offer some new ideas (based on age-old food traditions) of what to make and bring to a birthday, office party, holiday, or housewarming. Enjoy these sweets as a beautiful tribute to symmetry, balance, connection, and community.

CHIA SEED SMOOTHIE

Chia seeds aren't a newfound superfood, despite the recent buzz; the Chumash of California and the Tohono O'odham of the Sonoran Desert have harvested chia seeds for thousands of years, just as they've foraged for piñon nuts and acorns. Many of their traditional recipes include ground chia seeds, which is partially the inspiration for this smoothie. From there, I chose traditional ingredients from different regions (agave and blueberries), sticking to the basic Native American principle of incorporating nuts, seeds, and berries into recipes. With the exception of yogurt, almond milk, and ice, every ingredient here is one that Native Americans have been eating for centuries. I especially love the violet color of this filling, energy-boosting smoothie that won't spike your blood sugar.

Serves 1

1 tablespoon chia seeds, covered with water and allowed to expand for 30 minutes

½ cup (120 ml) almond milk

½ cup (120 ml) yogurt

2 tablespoons agave nectar

½ cup (75 g) blueberries

½ cup (120 ml) ice

In a blender, add the chia seeds, almond milk, yogurt, agave nectar, blueberries, and ice. Blend on high until smooth and serve.

CHOCOLATE AND PIÑON NUTCAKE

Baked goods aren't common in ancient Native American recipes, but they're essential to modern menus. This almost-flourless chocolate cake relies on traditional Indigenous ingredients like chocolate, berries, and piñon nuts, as well as nontraditional ingredients like eggs, flour, sugar, and brandy. Old meets new in this dense, decadent cake simply served with fresh berries in season. It's a personal favorite, one that I often make for small events and summer parties. Featuring chocolate in a dessert such as this is also a delicious way to emphasize the importance of cacao in Native American history. Chocolate is one of the most valuable and sought-after delicacies, and Indigenous communities first discovered and perfected its prized recipe. Today, chocolate remains an important food to the cultural and economic development of many Indigenous people.

Serves 6 to 8

1 cup (170 g) chopped bittersweet chocolate

½ cup (1 stick/115 g) unsalted butter

3 tablespoons brandy

1 teaspoon vanilla extract

1 teaspoon salt

½ cup (65 g) piñon nuts

2 tablespoons all-purpose flour

4 eggs, separated

¾ cup (150 g) sugar, or as needed

1 teaspoon cream of tartar

Fresh berries, for garnish, optional

Preheat the oven to 375°F (190°C). Grease and flour an 8-inch (20 cm) springform pan lined with parchment paper on the bottom.

In a double boiler over low heat, melt the chocolate and butter. Stir in the brandy, vanilla, and salt. Set aside.

In a food processor, add the piñon nuts and flour and pulse until just combined. Note: Do not process into a paste. Set aside.

In a medium bowl, add the egg whites, ¼ cup (50 g) of the sugar, and the cream of tartar. Using an electric mixer or good ol' fashioned elbow grease, mix or whisk to soft peaks. Set aside.

In another medium bowl, add the egg yolks and the remaining ½ cup (100 g) sugar and whisk until well incorporated. Note: The yolks should pour in the form of a ribbon, known as the ribbon stage. If they don't, whisk in a little more sugar.

Slowly whisk the hot chocolate mixture into the egg yolk mixture. Note: Whisk in slowly; if you add the hot chocolate all at once, the eggs will curdle. Next, fold in the flour mixture and finally the egg white mixture using a rubber spatula. Make sure the whites stay whipped.

Pour the batter in the prepared pan and bake until cooked through, 25 to 30 minutes. Remove from the oven and let cool before serving with berries (if using).

JUNEBERRY AND BLACKBERRY PUDDING
WITH LEMON AND AGAVE

During a recent culinary seminar in Los Angeles, I met a Sioux gentleman named Levi who introduced me to this traditional berry pudding. It's the perfect light dessert, he told me. It never fails to impress his friends and family. So here's the recipe he passed on to me, which I'm passing on to you. Don't let the name fool you—it's more like a summer fruit compote than a thick pudding. Like many Native American dishes, this one depends on finding ripe fruit in season.

Juneberries peak in June and July, and they're native to the upper Midwest of what's now the U.S. They look like blueberries but have a deeper, darker flavor along the lines of dark cherries or raisins. Substitute blueberries if you can't find juneberries—but if you can, make this pudding Levi's way. Serve it by itself, or however you'd most enjoy a berry compote: as a topping for scones, shortbread, rice pudding, yogurt, or ice cream.

Makes 10 (5- to 6-ounce/150 to 180 ml) servings

5 cups (725 g) juneberries (Saskatoon berries)

1 cup (140 g) blackberries

Zest and juice of 1 lemon

½ cup (120 ml) agave nectar

1 tablespoon cornstarch combined with 2 tablespoons water to create a slurry

In a saucepot over low heat, add the berries, lemon zest and juice, 2 cups (480 ml) water, and the agave nectar. Simmer for 45 minutes. Stir in the slurry until well incorporated. Remove from the heat and allow to cool before serving.

Sioux

The Sioux are a group of Great Plains people, including the Teton, Yankton, and Santee, whose lands extend north into what's now Canada. Originally from the northern region of the Mississippi River, the Sioux's expansive ancestral lands stretch across the areas now known as Iowa, Wisconsin, Kansas, Missouri, Minnesota, Nebraska, North Dakota, and South Dakota. The community has adopted the name Sioux, but it is not their word; they call themselves Lakota, Dakota, or Nakota, which all mean "allies."

According to Sioux beliefs, everything has spirit, or wakan. Wakan connects everything, from the earth to the animals to the water to the humans and their harvest. Their legends also include the story of a White Buffalo Calf Woman who gave the Sioux the sacred pipe that's used for ceremonies. She's described as incredibly beautiful, and the legend goes that she told the Sioux she would return again when the world was suffering. Before disappearing, she spun four times, changing each time into the colors of the four cardinal directions: white, yellow, red, and black. Afterward, great bison herds surrounded the Sioux, and ever since, whenever a bison is born it is read as a sign of answered prayers and a symbol of hope and the renewal of the life cycle.

Because bison were a central component of their lives, the Sioux became known for their hunting skills and traditional bison recipes—including pemmican, although their sweeter, toasted-cornmeal version is called wasná. In some regions, wedding wasná features a variety of dried berries like chokecherries, blueberries, and currants.

Today bison are still a central part of the Sioux's life and traditions, including the celebration of the first white bison born since 1933: in 1994, a white bison named Miracle was born in Wisconsin; another was born in Minnesota in 2012—both symbols of renewed hope.

ACCORDING TO SIOUX BELIEFS, EVERYTHING HAS SPIRIT, OR WAKAN.
WAKAN CONNECTS EVERYTHING, FROM THE EARTH TO THE ANIMALS
TO THE WATER TO THE HUMANS AND THEIR HARVEST.

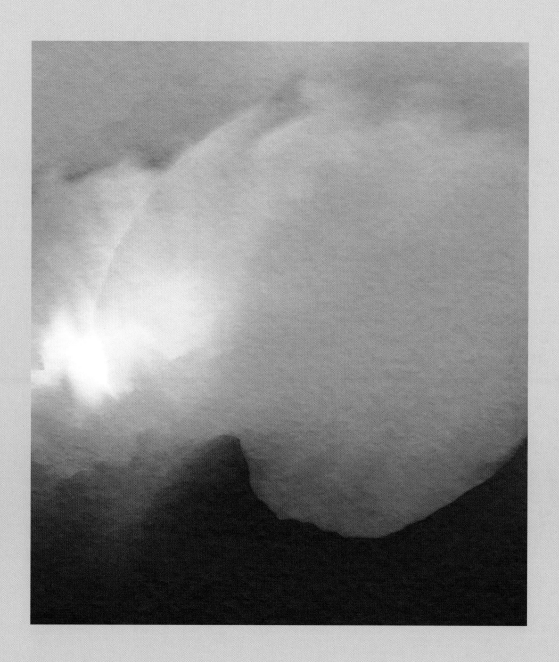

PRICKLY PEAR AND CHEESE MOUSSE TARTS

The only truly Native American elements of this tart are the fresh mint and prickly pear. For the prickly pear, the juice, syrup, and puree are all fairly easy to find—though you may need to plan ahead to make sure you have the prickly pear puree on hand. That desert fruit, with a taste that falls somewhere between a melon, plum, and strawberry, is what makes these tarts so unique and the mousse so delicious. Think of how it'll feel to serve this dessert to guests: a lighter version of the white chocolate cheesecake they may be used to, but with a tart, fruity sweetness they can't quite place.

Makes 12 (3-inch/7.5 cm) tarts

4½ ounces (125 g) white chocolate

12 ounces (340 g) cream cheese, softened

½ cup (100 g) sugar

1 cup (240 ml) prickly pear puree

2 sheets gelatin

Zest of 1 lemon

¼ cup (60 ml) limoncello liqueur

1½ teaspoons vanilla extract

2 cups (480 ml) heavy cream

12 (3-inch/7.5 cm) tart or sponge cake shells

Fresh mint leaves, for garnish

In a double boiler over low heat, melt the chocolate. Note: You can also melt the chocolate in the microwave. Microwave on high for 20-second intervals, stirring after each interval, until smooth. Remove the chocolate from the heat.

In a stand mixer, add the cream cheese, sugar, and prickly pear puree. Turn the mixer to medium speed to combine. With the mixer running, slowly add the melted chocolate.

In another double boiler over low heat, rehydrate the gelatin by submerging the sheets with the lemon zest, limoncello, and vanilla for 5 minutes. The sheets will become soft and springy. Add the cream cheese mixture and mix to combine.

In a large bowl, whip the cream to soft peaks. Using a rubber spatula, fold the whipped cream into the cream cheese mixture until incorporated. Do not overmix. Remove the mixture and pour into the tart shells (note: if your shells are a bit smaller, you may have some extra filling). Refrigerate the tarts until chilled. Garnish with mint leaves just before serving.

PUMPKIN BREAD PUDDING

Indigenous recipes did include lightly sweetened, spiced roasted squash, but pumpkin breads or pies didn't exist in traditional Native American recipes. If you're interested in a pumpkin dessert, I love this nutty, chocolatey, decadent bread pudding as a delicious alternative to the expected holiday pie. The pumpkin bread is delicious on its own, and as part of this pudding laced with chocolate and custard. If you've never had bread pudding, imagine eating just the warm, buttery, sweet insides of a stack of French toast. That's the general dessert experience. Now imagine that stack made of pumpkin bread, and you'll understand why this is one of my favorite autumnal desserts.

Serves 6 to 8

3 tablespoons unsalted butter

1 loaf Pumpkin Bread, cut into 1½-inch (4 cm) cubes, recipe follows

4 eggs, beaten

1 teaspoon salt

¾ cup (150 g) sugar

1 teaspoon vanilla extract

4 cups (960 ml) whole milk

1 cup (175 g) semisweet chocolate chips

Grease a 9-inch (23 cm) square baking dish with the butter. Arrange the diced pumpkin bread evenly in the dish and set aside.

In a large bowl, whisk the eggs, salt, sugar, and vanilla until well incorporated. Set aside.

In a small saucepot over medium heat, bring the milk to a heavy simmer. Once simmering, slowly whisk the hot milk into the egg mixture. Note: Whisk in slowly; if you add the hot milk all at once, the eggs will curdle. Slowly pour over the pumpkin bread. Make sure all the bread is soaked with the mixture. Sprinkle the chocolate chips evenly over the top. Transfer to the refrigerator for about 2 hours.

When ready to bake, preheat the oven to 350°F (175°C).

Prepare a water bath by setting the baking dish into a larger ovenproof pan and pouring hot water into the ovenproof pan to come halfway up the sides of the baking dish. Carefully transfer to the oven and bake the pudding for 45 to 50 minutes, or until cooked through. Remove from the oven and serve warm.

PUMPKIN BREAD
Makes 1 loaf

1½ cups (190 g) all-purpose flour

½ teaspoon salt

1 cup (200 g) sugar

1 teaspoon baking soda

1 cup (240 ml) pumpkin puree

½ cup (120 ml) vegetable oil

2 eggs, beaten

½ teaspoon grated fresh nutmeg

½ teaspoon ground cinnamon

½ teaspoon ground allspice

½ cup (60 g) chopped walnuts

2 tablespoons unsalted butter

Preheat the oven to 350°F (175°C).

In a medium bowl, sift the flour, salt, sugar, and baking soda together. In another bowl, add ¼ cup (60 ml) water, the pumpkin puree, oil, eggs, nutmeg, cinnamon, and allspice. Stir well to combine. Whisk the dry ingredients into the pumpkin mixture, then stir in the walnuts. Grease a standard (8½ by 4½ by 2½-inch/21 by 11 by 6 cm) loaf pan with the butter. Pour the mixture into the pan and place on a baking sheet. Transfer to the oven and bake 50 to 60 minutes, or until cooked through. Remove from the oven and let cool.

Loaf of pumpkin bread

PUMPKIN BREAD PUDDING

RICE PUDDING WITH CRANBERRY

Unlike the wild manoomin rice of Minnesota (see pages 78 and 82), white rice isn't a traditional ingredient in Native American cuisine. It came to this continent in the late 1600s, and first flourished in what's now South Carolina, eventually making its way into Native American recipes. I've included rice pudding here because it's one of my favorites for a brisk fall or winter afternoon. It's also the perfect way to create a sweet, comforting treat from something I've already got on hand. I top my rice pudding with cranberry sauce instead of the more common raisins. Tart berries complement the sweet pudding and add a Native American touch to a non-Native recipe. If summer berries are in season when you decide to make this dessert, sprinkle those on top instead. Or top it with the Juneberry and Blackberry Pudding with Lemon and Agave (page 256).

Serves 4

¾ cup (150 g) short-grain white rice

2 cups (480 ml) whole milk

1 teaspoon salt

¼ cup (60 ml) agave nectar

1 teaspoon vanilla extract

Cranberry Sauce, for garnish, recipe follows

In a medium saucepot over medium heat, add the rice and milk and bring to a simmer. Reduce the heat to low, cover, and simmer for 10 minutes. Fluff the rice with a fork and add the salt, agave nectar, and vanilla. Continue to stir, which activates the starch. Allow to simmer for another 5 minutes. Remove from the heat and serve with warm cranberry sauce.

CRANBERRY SAUCE
Makes approximately 2 cups (480 ml)

2 cups (190 g) fresh or frozen cranberries

2 cups (480 ml) orange juice

Zest and juice of 1 lemon

In a medium saucepan over medium heat, add the cranberries, orange juice, lemon zest, and lemon juice. Stir well to combine. Cook until the cranberries break down, about 20 minutes. Serve warm.

STEAMED INDIAN CORN PUDDING

I've adapted this dish from a recipe first made popular by English settlers in the colonial era of the U.S. It's a traditional American dessert with Native American roots. The English, craving the sweetened porridge they called hasty pudding, began using Native American cornmeal (which they called Indian meal) to create a similar porridge sweetened with milk and molasses. My version takes the idea fully into the modern age.

It's not a porridge but a silky-smooth, creamy baked custard. I keep the traditional flavors of molasses and corn but remove any hint of grittiness and add dashes of fragrant cinnamon and nutmeg plus a bright taste of cranberry. To break from tradition even further, I serve this pudding with a scoop of ice cream. But there's no reason you shouldn't also enjoy it as a comforting treat on a lazy morning with a fresh cup of coffee.

Serves 6 to 8

6 cups (1.4 L) whole milk

½ cup (1 stick/115 g) unsalted butter

3 eggs, beaten

½ cup (120 ml) molasses

⅓ cup (65 g) sugar

1 teaspoon cinnamon

1 teaspoon grated fresh nutmeg

½ cup (90 g) yellow cornmeal

¼ cup (30 g) all-purpose flour

1 teaspoon salt

1 cup (140 g) dried cranberries

Vanilla ice cream, for serving, optional

Fresh cranberries, for garnish, optional

Preheat the oven to 300°F (150°C).

In a heavy-bottom pot over medium heat, add the milk and butter and bring to a rapid simmer.

While the milk comes to a simmer, in a large bowl, whisk together the eggs, molasses, sugar, cinnamon, and nutmeg. In another bowl, whisk together the cornmeal, flour, and salt.

Once the milk and butter come to a rapid simmer, remove from the heat and slowly whisk into the bowl with the eggs. Note: Whisk in slowly; if you add the hot milk all at once, the eggs will curdle. After the milk and butter are incorporated into the egg mixture, whisk in the flour-cornmeal mixture. After everything is incorporated, stir in the dried cranberries.

Pour the mixture into a 12-inch (30.5 cm) round baking dish or pan. Note: If you prefer using a water bath during the baking process (often used to keep baked items very moist), set the baking dish into a larger ovenproof pan and pour hot water into the ovenproof pan to come halfway up the sides of the baking dish. Carefully transfer to the oven and bake until cooked through, about 90 minutes. Remove from the oven and serve warm with ice cream (if using). Garnish with fresh cranberries, if desired.

SUMMER PEACH CRISP

Nothing says summer quite like a perfectly ripe, juicy peach—and while neither the fruit nor this recipe is traditionally Native American, I love this crisp, adapted from a recipe I first tasted at a Cherokee-hosted event; it celebrates the seasonal harvest, it's incredibly tasty, and it honors the Cherokee communities who have been growing peaches in Georgia for generations. To make this recipe the way it should taste, find the freshest, ripest peaches possible, preferably grown locally in the height of late summer. Immerse yourself in the sweet-nutty-juicy-crunchy combination of peaches and pecans and the play of textures in the brown sugar crust. Serve warm.

Serves 6 to 8

For the peach filling:

4 fresh peaches, or 1 pound (455 g) frozen

3 tablespoons unsalted butter

½ cup (120 ml) agave nectar or ½ cup (110 g) packed brown sugar

2 whole cloves, wrapped and tied in cheesecloth

1 teaspoon cinnamon

½ teaspoon grated fresh nutmeg

1 tablespoon cornstarch

For the crust:

½ cup (110 g) packed brown sugar

½ cup (65 g) all-purpose flour

2 cups (180 g) old-fashioned oats

¼ cup (30 g) chopped pecans, optional

Zest of 1 lemon

2 teaspoons salt

¼ cup (60 ml) whole milk

¼ cup (55 g) unsalted butter, diced

Make the peach filling: If using fresh peaches, bring a pot of water to a boil. Using a paring knife, slice an X on the bottom of each peach (the side opposite the stem). Be careful not to penetrate deep into the flesh. Fill a bowl with ice and water and set aside. Place the peaches in the boiling water for about 45 seconds and then remove and immediately plunge the peaches into the ice water. The skins should now be easy to peel. Once peeled, cut the peaches in half, remove the pits, and slice each half into wedges. Set aside.

In a 12-inch (30.5 cm) cast-iron skillet, Dutch oven, or casserole dish over medium heat, add 3 tablespoons butter. When the butter is melted, add the peaches, agave nectar, cloves, cinnamon, nutmeg, and cornstarch. Cook, stirring often, until the peaches are soft and the mixture is thick. Remove from the heat and discard the clove satchel. Set aside.

Preheat the oven to 350°F (175°C).

Make the crust: In a medium bowl, add the brown sugar, flour, oats, pecans (if using), lemon zest, salt, and milk and stir well to combine. Spread the crust mixture atop the peaches in the cast-iron skillet. Top the crust with ¼ cup (55 g) diced butter. Transfer the skillet to the oven and bake for 40 to 50 minutes, or until the crust is cooked through and golden brown. Note: For easy oven cleanup, place the skillet on a baking sheet in the oven. Remove the skillet from the oven and serve.

Cherokee

Although *Cherokee* is a Muscogee word, it's been adopted by the people and affiliated bands from Georgia, Virginia, Kentucky, Tennessee, and the Carolinas. Aniyunwiya is the community's name in Tsalagi, their own language.

The ancestral region of the Cherokee in the Appalachians influences their diverse diet of pumpkins and other squashes, dried fruit, corn, potatoes, and beans, grown using the three sisters method of planting squash, beans, and corn together. The predominant ancestral Cherokee corn is flint corn, named for the hard texture of its kernels; it doesn't always get dry and hot enough in the Southeast for softer corn varieties to grow.

With the beans that climbed the corn stalks, the ancestral Cherokee would prepare bean bread, also known as broadsword because of its flat, rectangular shape. The beans are mashed into a dough, which is wrapped in corn husks and steamed like dumplings or tamales. Traditional protein sources include wild game like deer, fowl, hogs, and buffalo. And when hunters returned home, they'd celebrate with a feast.

They also would dry meats and fruit for the winter, to enjoy the flavors of summer year-round. To do this traditionally, in the sun, they'd have to study the clouds to make sure it wouldn't rain on the food they were hoping to preserve. In the rich hills of the Appalachians, the Cherokee also maintained orchards of chestnuts, walnuts, and pecans.

The Cherokee are also known for playing a marble game somewhat similar to croquet and bocce. Using stone marbles roughly the size of billiard balls, players attempt to get their marble in a hole while thwarting their opponents and knocking away their marbles. In addition to marbles, Cherokee have been playing stickball for centuries. Often, before a match, there will be traditional dances. Like in most cultures, sports are a communal social event for Cherokee and an excuse to celebrate—and eat.

LIKE IN MOST CULTURES, SPORTS ARE A COMMUNAL SOCIAL EVENT
FOR CHEROKEE AND AN EXCUSE TO CELEBRATE—AND EAT.

TOASTED BLUE CORNMEAL ^{WITH} MIXED BERRIES ^{AND} AGAVE

I've talked a lot in this book about the creativity involved in Native American recipes; this classic Navajo porridge is an example of that principle. It takes a common ingredient, cornmeal, and creates a dessert, rather than a savory side dish, a dumpling, or a crust for fish or meat. When I was a kid, I'd eat this sweet cornmeal drizzled with honey, berries, and milk at any time of day: breakfast, lunch, dinner, or dessert. Culinary ash, which Navajos make by burning juniper trees, adds a smoky flavor to the toasted cornmeal and also brightens the blue color. If you don't like smoke and sweetness together, use baking powder instead. Drizzle with your favorite sweetener to balance the hint of smoke, the nuttiness of the toasted corn, and the tart, fresh berries.

Serves 4 to 6

1 cup (120 g) blue cornmeal

1½ teaspoons culinary ash or baking powder

Whole milk (about ½ cup/120 ml per serving), for garnish

1 cup (140 g) mixed fresh berries, for garnish

Agave nectar, for garnish

In a medium skillet over high heat, add the cornmeal. Stir constantly until the cornmeal is lightly browned, about 5 minutes. Remove from the heat and set aside.

In a medium saucepot, add 4 cups (960 ml) water and bring to a boil over high heat. Slowly add the toasted cornmeal and culinary ash while stirring. Reduce the heat to medium-low and continue to stir until the cornmeal begins to pull away from the sides of the pot. Remove from the heat and serve hot in individual serving bowls topped with milk, berries, and a drizzle of agave nectar.

WARM APPLE BREAD PUDDING

For five hundred years or so, Native American communities across the nation have incorporated apples into their recipes. In this book, you've seen apples with wild rice, seafood, vegetables, and meats, and finally in dessert. Try this cozy, custardy, caramelized apple bread pudding in midwinter—though I won't stop you from making it in spring, summer, or fall. Bread pudding is far from traditional Indigenous cuisine, but I like it as a delicious change from typical cakes and pies.

Serves 6 to 8

2 Granny Smith apples, cored and diced

1½ cups (300 g) sugar

4½ tablespoons (65 g) unsalted butter plus 3 tablespoons for greasing the pan

3 cups (720 ml) whole milk

1 small vanilla bean or 1 teaspoon vanilla extract

1 cup (240 ml) applesauce

¼ teaspoon cinnamon

¼ teaspoon grated fresh nutmeg

3 eggs, beaten

9 cups (400 g) cubed day-old French bread (one loaf cut into 1½-inch/4 cm cubes)

In a medium bowl, add the apple pieces and toss with ½ cup (100 g) of the sugar. Set aside.

In a large sauté pan over low heat, add 1½ tablespoons of the butter. When the butter is melted, add the sugar-coated apples and sauté for 15 minutes, covered. Remove the lid and allow the apples to caramelize, about 5 minutes. Remove from the heat and set aside.

In a medium saucepan over low heat, add the milk. Split the vanilla bean and, with a sharp knife, scrape the inside of the bean and remove the seeds. Add the seeds to the milk. If using vanilla extract, simply add to the milk. Stir in the remaining 1 cup (200 g) sugar along with the applesauce, cinnamon, and nutmeg. Stir until the sugar is dissolved into the warm milk, then remove the milk from the heat. Very slowly whisk in the eggs. Note: Do not pour the eggs into the milk all at once or they will curdle.

Grease a 9 by 13-inch (23 by 33 cm) baking pan with 3 tablespoons of the butter. Arrange the bread cubes on the bottom of the pan, then spoon the caramelized apples evenly over the bread. Pour the custard evenly over the apples and bread. Refrigerate the pan for 30 minutes to 1 hour.

Preheat the oven to 350°F (175°C).

Prepare a water bath by setting the baking pan into a larger ovenproof pan and pouring hot water into the ovenproof pan to come halfway up the sides of the baking pan. Cut the remaining 3 tablespoons butter into cubes and place them all over the bread pudding. Carefully transfer to the oven and bake for 1 hour, or until the pudding is set and the top is lightly brown. Remove from the oven and allow to cool for a few minutes before serving.

Further Reading

For those interested in America's Native heritage, from Indigenous foods and early agriculture to historical moments and family celebrations, I recommend reading as much as you can, exploring the work of a variety of authors. Over the years, I've amassed a collection of fascinating books about Native American culture, from light, entertaining reads that discuss food and celebrations to deep historical explorations of the American Indian and the origins of myths and legends. These titles open the doors to many stories about the way of life for America's Indigenous peoples, all the while emphasizing the importance of Native American advancement, triumph, tragedy, resistance, and courage.

Food and Agriculture

Caduto, Michael J. *Native American Gardening: Stories, Projects and Recipes for Families*. Wheat Ridge, Colorado: Fulcrum Publishing, 1996.

Fritz, Gayle J. *Feeding Cahokia: Early Agriculture in the North American Heartland.* Tuscaloosa: University of Alabama Press, 2019.

Hurt, R. Douglas. *Indian Agriculture in America: Prehistory to the Present.* Lawrence: University Press of Kansas, 1988.

Nabhan, Gary Paul. Enduring Seeds: *Native American Agriculture and Wild Plant Conservation.* Tucson: University of Arizona Press, 2002.

Salmon, Enrique. *Eating the Landscape: American Indian Stories of Food, Identity, and Resilience.* Tucson: University of Arizona Press, 2012.

Weatherford, Jack. *Indian Givers: How Native Americans Transformed the World.* New York: Three Rivers Press, 2010.

Wilson, Gilbert L. *Native American Gardening: Buffalobird-Woman's Guide to Traditional Methods.* Mineola, New York: Dover Publications, 2005.

Celebration

Mikoley, Kate. *Native American Ceremonies and Celebrations: From Potlatches to Powwows.* New York: Gareth Stevens Publishing, 2018.

Pheasant-Neganigwane, Karen. *Powwow: A Celebration through Song and Dance.* Victoria, British Columbia: Orca Book Publishers, 2020.

History

Brown, Dee. *Bury My Heart at Wounded Knee: An Indian History of the American West.* New York: Henry Holt and Company, 2007.

Deloria, Vine, Jr. *Custer Died for Your Sins: An Indian Manifesto.* Norman: University of Oklahoma Press, 1988.

Drury, Bob, and Tom Clavin. *The Heart of Everything That Is: The Untold Story of Red Cloud, An American Legend.* New York: Simon & Schuster, 2014.

Dunbar-Ortiz, Roxanne. *An Indigenous Peoples' History of the United States.* Boston: Beacon Press, 2015.

Ehle, John. *Trail of Tears: The Rise and Fall of the Cherokee Nation.* New York: Doubleday, 1988.

Erdoes, Richard, and Alfonso Ortiz, eds. *American Indian: Myths and Legends.* New York: Pantheon Books, 1984.

Gwynne, S. C. *Empire of the Summer Moon: Quanah Parker and the Rise and Fall of the Comanches, the Most Powerful Indian Tribe in American History.* New York: Scribner, 2010.

Hayes, Ernestine. *The Tao of Raven: An Alaska Native Memoir.* Seattle: University of Washington Press, 2019.

Las Casas, Bartolomé de. Edited and translated by Nigel Griffin. *A Short Account of the Destruction of the Indies.* New York: Penguin Books, 1992.

Mann, Charles C. *1491: New Revelations of the Americas Before Columbus.* New York: Vintage Books, 2006.

Miranda, Deborah A. *Bad Indians: A Tribal Memoir.* Berkeley, CA: Heyday, 2013.

Smith, Paul Chaat. *Everything You Know about Indians Is Wrong.* Minneapolis: University of Minnesota Press, 2009.

Treuer, David. *The Heartbeat of Wounded Knee: Native America from 1890 to the Present.* New York: Riverhead Books, 2019.

Acknowledgments

The authors would like to thank the following individuals for their help and support with this cookbook:

Freddie

My mother, who did me a favor by helping me get into culinary school, and for allowing me to use her home as an office to write all the recipes for this book.

My stepfather, Henry Long, and my sister, Jacy Lee, for their continued support. My nephew Jacob W. Bitsoie, who keeps me working as hard as I can. Charlie and J.J. Lee, Alyson, and Marriah. Thank you! And Jayme Brown for never giving up on me.

Paul Zemitzsch for connecting me with James O. Fraioli, otherwise this project would never have been possible.

Adam Beach, who has been a part of my career since the beginning and has been a very strong supporter of me and my work.

Robert Platero, Jeff Grey, Ryan Jones, Juan Barajas, Shane Plumer, and David Lazo for incredible amounts of personal support.

Twila Casadore, my desert guild and food historian.

Sensitivity reader C. Cali Martin (Osage/Kaw).

I would also like to personally thank my colleagues and friends at Restaurant Associates for the many opportunities, especially Albert Lukas and George Conomos. Also, the Phoenix Indian School Visitor Center and Rosalie Talahongva and Patty Talahongva of Indian Country Today.

Last but not least, Thom Denomme, who has been with me from the start.

James

Laura Dozier, Jennifer Wagner, and the wonderful editorial and creative teams at Abrams.

Paul Zemitzsch and Explore Green.

Food photographer Quentin Bacon and food stylist Paul Grimes.

Literary wizards Nicole Hardy and Kate Fiduccia.

My loving wife, Tiffany Fraioli, for her constant love and support.

INDEX

Editor: Laura Dozier
Designer: Jennifer Wagner
Production Manager: Denise LaCongo

Library of Congress Control Number: 2021932551

ISBN: 978-1-4197-5355-8
eISBN: 978-1-64700-252-7

ABRAMS The Art of Books
195 Broadway, New York, NY 10007
abramsbooks.com